YOUNG
ALCOHOLICS

by
Tom Alibrandi

Published by

CompCare® publications

2415 Annapolis Lane, Suite 140, Minneapolis, Minnesota 55441
A division of Comprehensive Care Corporation

(Ask for our catalog, 800/328-3330, toll free outside Minnesota or 612/559-4800, Minnesota residents)

Library of Congress Catalog Card
No. 77-87741
ISBN No. 0-89638-014-9

YOUNG
ALCOHOLICS

For Astrid, whose light fell across me
and I'll never be the same.

Acknowledgments

To Doug Chalmers, whose work in the field of adolescent alcoholism has made certain sections of this book possible.

To Liz Breen, who proofread the manuscript.

To Jane Thomas Noland for her work in editing this book.

To all my brothers and sisters who stepped from the curb into addiction before finding the sunny side of the street. And to those who never found it.

Contents

Child of Pain

I see you every day
young eyes
unlined faces
cornered smiles
walls of words
looks that demand
prove it
show me a better way.

Blindly following
asphalt sages
left to the electronic classroom
where you've learned well
to deaden those words of hurt,
mommy's too stoned to love me
daddy's busy at work.

Through cool and crowded
aloneness
games of escape you've learned
there's a force in you
like me
crying to be
set free.

Child of pain
child of craving
can you see
the blueprint to be free?
How far must you go
where winds of sadness
don't blow?

From *Hallways*
by Tom Alibrandi
1978, Chicken Walk Books

The names of all persons whose stories are told briefly in this book have been changed to protect their anonymity.

In order to make this printing even more valuable to parents, counselors and educators, a few changes have been made in some of the questionnaires. Such changes are based on further testing and clinical studies.

YOUNG
ALCOHOLICS

About Youth and Drinking

Fact: A 1976 study conducted by the Alcoholism Council of Orange County, California, showed that two thirds of the 2,500 polled—aged seven to twenty-one—had reached "drinker status," that is, they have had more than two or three drinks in their lives. This is identical to the drinking rate among adults in a 1965 sample.

Fact: The same survey showed that eighty-five percent of eleventh and twelfth graders drink alcohol at least occasionally. This is almost a four hundred percent increase over a youth drinking patterns study done in 1964. By the time an alcohol-abusing youth reaches college age, there is a forty-two percent chance that he or she already is drinking out of control.

Fact: A San Mateo County, California, study in 1975 reported that the use of barbiturates, amphetamines, LSD, heroin and other nonprescription "hard drugs" by students in grades seven through twelve had decreased during the previous five years.

Fact: The Orange County survey of youth drinking patterns shows that six percent of the children aged seven through eleven who were polled already are showing early signs of alcoholism.

Fact: In the same survey, only twenty-five percent of those questioned favored pot over alcohol. While eighty-five percent drink alcohol, "only" twenty-nine percent use other drugs. (Some of the alcohol drinkers also use other drugs.)

Fact: Sixty percent of the people killed in drunk driving accidents are in their teens. Nearly 20,000 teenagers are killed annually because of drunken driving.

Fact: The National Institute on Alcohol Abuse and Alcoholism (NIAAA) reports that 1.3 million Americans between the ages of twelve and seventeen have serious drinking problems. Recent studies indicate the NIAAA's figures are understated. In addition, the NIAAA has failed to take into account youngsters under age twelve, whose drinking, as shown in the Orange County survey, has reached problem levels.

Fact: In the United States, arrests of teenagers for drunk driving have tripled since 1960.

Fact: National suicide rates among grade-school-age youngsters have risen sharply. Depression has been cited as the major reason preteens take their own lives. *Alcohol is a depressant drug.* In the Orange County survey, twenty-six percent of those questioned in grades three through eight drink alcohol, at least occasionally. Nearly twelve percent have reached problem proportions in their drinking. The suicide rate for alcoholics is fifty-eight times that of non-alcoholics.

Fact: Almost thirty percent of the youngsters who drink, according to the Orange County survey, stated they drank the depressant drug alcohol in order to: 1)"cheer me up when I'm in a bad mood"; 2) "change the way I feel"; 3) "feel more relaxed with the opposite sex"; 4) "feel more at ease with people." *Alcohol is a depressant drug.*

Fact: According to reports published in the Los Angeles *Times*, the national sales of pop wines (alcoholic beverages marketed for youth) reached thirty-three million gallons in 1974—an increase of thirty million gallons in seven years.

vi.

Fact: According to the Orange County, California, Criminal Justice Council, the juvenile arrest rate is nearly two-and-one-half times the adult arrest rate.

Fact: A member of the Orange County Public Defenders Office stated publicly that virtually *every* juvenile his office defended in 1976 claimed to have been drinking alcohol when they committed the crime for which they were being tried.

Fact: A recent poll conducted by the director of Joplin Boys' Ranch (an Orange County juvenile detention camp), showed that ninety-eight out of one hundred boys in camp were drinking when they committed the offense that put them in closed care.

Fact: Americans consumed 4.6 billion gallons of beer and ale in 1976. Ninety-five million Americans (including teens) drink alcohol. On the average, each person who drinks alcohol consumes nearly forty-nine gallons of beer annually. In addition, each drinking person downs in excess of twenty-nine fifths of liquor and thirty fifths of wine per year.

Fact: Truancy among high school students in most areas of the country has risen. According to schools' records in Orange County, truancy increased almost four hundred percent in the school year 1975-76. According to NIAAA statistics, youths who are frequently truant from school are considered at high risk for developing alcohol problems, or they have already reached problem proportions in their drinking.

Fact: Young alcoholics come from upper-middle-class families as well as from ghetto or barrio areas. Alcoholism knows no social, economic or age distinctions. Nor does it differentiate by gender (equal numbers of young females and males abuse alcohol). Parents' divorce decrees—or lack of them—don't seem to have any effect on whether children become alcoholic, either. A youngster from a two-parent home has as great a chance of becoming an alcoholic as a kid from a one-parent family.

According to an NIAAA study, in terms of ethnic background, Native American youths have the highest proportion (16.5 percent) of "heavy drinkers," (defined as those who drink alcohol at least once a week and have five to twelve drinks per occasion.) They are followed by Orientals (13.5 percent), Spanish (10.9 percent), Whites (10.7 percent) and Blacks (5.7 percent).

Part One

Youth Alcoholism:
A Growing Problem

1

The New Skid Row: Wherever Kids Hang Out

"Alcoholism is even a bigger problem than drugs among the kids." Henry (The Fonz) Winkler, on vetoing Falstaff's drinking scene for his March 1977 TV special, *Henry Winkler Meets William Shakespeare.*

☆   ☆   ☆

"This spring they (kids) are more interested in beer and the beach than drugs and demonstrations.

"A few years ago, arrests averaged fifty to seventy-five a day, mostly on drug charges. Today, they're averaging eight to ten daily, mostly for disorderly intoxication.

"'Basically, they're back to beer and sex,' Ed DelaVergue, a city public information officer, said. 'They're down here for a suntan, booze ... It's come full circle in the past fifteen to twenty years.'" From an article in the Los Angeles *Times,* March 1977, commenting on the rush of young people to Fort Lauderdale, Florida, during spring recess.

☆　☆　☆

"Just because drinking and sex can be fun does not mean that alcoholism and syphilis are not diseases," Dr. D. K. Chalmers, *The Alcoholic's Controlled Drinking Time.*

☆　☆　☆

Mike, at seventeen, appeared to have everything going for him. A senior in high school, he planned to attend junior college in the fall, had a part-time job and a steady girl friend. Mike seemed, to an outsider, to be well-adjusted and happy—except for one problem, which his parents had struggled to keep secret. He had been arrested twice for driving under the influence of alcohol.

Mike's run-in with the law, when all else was going well for him, puzzled and infuriated his father, a computer technician, and his mother, a grade-school teacher. They had become particularly alarmed when their son grew progressively more depressed and withdrew from family activities. They took him to a psychiatrist who had been recommended by Mike's school counselor. The doctor prescribed the tranquilizer Valium, reporting that the boy was nervous and took things too seriously.

Returning from school one afternoon, Mike's mother found him hanging in the garage, the victim of suicide. The number of teens and preteens who take their own lives is becoming a frightening statistic. Mike was an alcoholic.

☆　☆　☆

Carla was having trouble handling her responsibilities. She had fallen behind in her school work and was reported truant six times before the school year was half over. She was not getting home on time. She had been placed on juvenile probation for shoplifting from a neighborhood grocery store.

At a loss to explain her daughter's behavior, Carla's mother took her to their family physician for a general examination. After discovering the beginnings of a stomach ulcer, the doctor learned a startling fact—a replay of a situation he had been seeing with increasing frequency over the past few years. Carla had been stealing liquor from her unsuspecting parents for over three years. She was seriously abusing alcohol, already experiencing blackouts, alienated from some of her friends because of drinking, and now she had the beginnings of an ulcer. Carla is an alcoholic. She is twelve years old.

Carla comes to our Orange County Alcoholism Council's youth group and has also joined a young people's group of Alcoholics Anonymous (AA). She has been free from alcohol and other drugs for three months, is no longer truant, gets along with her friends again and is following her parents' instructions. Her probation officer has told her that if she can maintain this record, she will be released from juvenile probation within three months.

To witness the love and hope in Carla's eyes, where there was only arrogance and fear, to hear her parents share the joy of watching their daughter grow as a human being, to see Carla as a positive influence on other members of our group —all this offers solid testimony that there is a way back for young alcoholics. They do not have to be shrugged off or thrown aside by society, parents or themselves. There are alternatives for the young alcohol abuser. There is hope.

☆   ☆   ☆

These stories are not exceptional. Nor are they fictitious. These two—and the others mentioned in this book—are among over one thousand youngsters I have come to know as Director of Youth Programs of the Alcoholism Council of Orange County, California. They are runaways, truants, probation cases, suicide attempts, incorrigibles and drunk drivers—all with one common denominator. They are

3

youngsters between the ages of seven and twenty-one with serious drinking problems. Some are arrogant, some battered. All are suffering chronic physical and emotional damage from alcohol, clearly the drug of choice among today's youth. These are youngsters whose drinking has so interfered with their lives that they have been sent to our program for help.

Stories like Carla's and Mike's are all too real. They are happening all over our country.

What can parents, teachers, counselors, law enforcement officers, juvenile justice authorities, public officials and young people themselves do to combat the problem of youth alcoholism?

Although there are still many things about addiction and its treatment that are not understood—particularly when it involves youth—some beginnings have been made.

It is my hope that this book will provide some answers.

I have wanted to write it for some time, since youth alcoholism is a subject close to me. Having worked in the field of addictions for over ten years, I have seen literally thousands of preteens and teens hand out pieces of their freedom, inner and outer, because they are abusing alcohol.

These young people, like all adolescents, are crying for freedom. Instead they become enslaved by alcoholism. They lose their independence to the restrictions of parental distrust, physical impairments, revocation of drivers' licenses, juvenile probation—even jail. Positive relationships disappear. Educational horizons narrow. In fact, all of life's potential diminishes for young alcoholics.

There are also inner losses of freedom. As a young person's addiction to alcohol grows, self-worth evaporates and ambition disappears. The young alcoholic enters an emotional prison. He or she becomes locked into self-loathing, fear, guilt, remorse and increasing dependence on the drug, alcohol.

An alcoholic youngster develops into a dishonest, self-obsessed and petty kid who continually finds himself or herself in a tangle of trouble, in the home or the community or both, difficulties that are often blamed on others.

Whenever the word "alcoholic" is mentioned, most people automatically think "skid row" or "wino." An alcoholic soon finds skid row to be a subjective place, a state of mind, just as freedom is. A preteen or teen can be on skid row of the soul while standing in the living room of the family's $100,000 house.

Alcoholism among this country's youth has risen sharply during the last decade, over 300 percent, according to recent studies. This confirms what youth counselors and juvenile justice officers have come to know through experience: More kids are drinking—and drinking more—than ever before. Or, in the words of one counselor, "Kids are drinking their brains out."

A recent survey conducted by the Alcoholism Council of Orange County, California,* showed that for twenty-seven percent of the 2,500 youngsters questioned, between the ages of seven and twenty-one, drinking already has reached alcoholic proportions. This means that over one fourth of the kids who drink are no longer social drinkers (many never were), but are early, middle or late stage alcoholics. That is, they use beer, wine or hard liquor to the extent that it seriously and consistently interferes with one or more areas of their lives.**

This same survey tells us that eighty-three percent of the total questioned drink alcohol, in varying amounts, with varying frequency, and that by the time an alcohol-abusing youngster reaches college, there is a forty-two percent chance that he or she already is drinking out of control. This startling rate is fifty percent greater than the national percentage of drinking in adult males in 1965.

---

*The study, *A Survey of Drinking Patterns and Problem Drinking Among Youth in Orange County*, is included in Part Two of this book.

**Jellinek, E. M., *Disease Concept of Alcoholism*, New Haven, 1960, United Printing Service.

And these figures are not confined to Southern California. One recent study in Massachusetts showed that, of the high school students questioned, 92.7 percent drink alcohol and 59.4 percent get drunk regularly.

A 1975 San Mateo County, California survey indicated that 86.3 percent of the youths who drink, do so "weekly or more frequently." This is almost double the rate of "weekly or more" users in 1970 in the same school districts.

In Maryland, eighty-four percent of eleventh graders tested use alcohol.

In New York, sixty percent of high-school-age young people questioned admitted regular use of alcohol.

In Colorado, eighty percent of those tested in selected school districts in the fifth grade and up use alcohol.

In Illinois, 42.6 percent of high-school-age youngsters surveyed qualified as problem drinkers.

During the early 1970s, the National Council on Alcoholism estimated that there were 17,500 teenage alcoholics in Orange County. Based upon our recent survey, there are probably around 43,000 youngsters aged fourteen through seventeen who have reached at least beginning or early stage alcoholism. And that figure does not include the increasing number of problem drinkers under the age of fourteen.

Experience has shown that, in most cases, young alcoholics are gravely misdiagnosed. Most adults wouldn't know a young alcoholic if the kid hit them with a truck (not such an unlikely happening at that, if the young person is an alcohol abuser who also drives a truck). So it becomes a question of first educating adults as to what their children are into. How to help problem-drinking children is another question, one that is only beginning to have some answers.

The disease of alcoholism in teenagers needs to be called by its right name. When it is not—when parents, teachers or members of the clergy moralize and chastise—the young alcoholic becomes further alienated from a community he or she has become less and less a part of anyway.

A young person's drinking problem often is regarded as a matter of will power, if indeed it is recognized as a problem at all. Friends, parents and society offer differing and confusing data about what an acceptable "drinking norm" may be.

Those who treat young alcoholics—doctors, school nurses and mental health workers—have been confronted with a frightening reality: *The physical and emotional damage caused by alcohol in teen and preteen abusers seems to occur sooner than it does in their adult counterparts.* A developing young body seems less capable of handling alcohol abuse than a mature one. Physical and emotional manifestations of alcohol abuse seem more pronounced among youth, showing up in less time and from smaller quantities than among adults.

The *Journal of Safety Research* (1973) hinted at this phenomenon in a study of youths who drink and drive. They stated that certain concentrations of alcohol in the bloodstream are important factors in accidents among teenagers. Among adults aged twenty-five through sixty-nine, identical concentrations are not significant.

Certain physical disorders resulting from alcohol abuse, heretofore associated with the long-term, rusty-zipper and yellow-shoe alcoholic, are becoming more evident among teen and preteen drinkers, even after a few years, or only a few months, of abusing alcohol.

There is a documented case of one nine-year-old boy in Nebraska, who, when it was discovered that he had been drinking steadily for three years, was admitted to a hospital for treatment of severe delirium tremens (DT's). Another nine-year-old in Los Angeles died in late 1976 from alcohol-induced cirrhosis of the liver.

Professionals in the field of alcoholism treatment are becoming alarmed as they see youngsters as young as eight —with relatively short histories of abusing alcohol—who are already suffering from ulcers, cirrhosis of the liver, pancreatitis, malnutrition and other ailments related to problem drinking. Reasons for this are still unclear, but the fact remains that when a kid abuses alcohol regularly, her or his body tends to go "tilt." Developing organs and nervous systems appear unable to cope with heavy drinking.

And what about the families of young alcoholics, since alcoholism is a disease that affects the whole family? By the time a young person reaches a problem stage in drinking, the family is a wreck, operating out of fear, anger or disgust or all three. Parents are anxious and confused. They have lost control of their household—so accustomed to operating around the poor decisions and behavior of the problem-drinking youth that they are living in their alcohol-abusing offspring's house, rather than vice versa. The house is a battleground, and it's the parents who are getting the worst of it, trying to combat the situation on their child's terms.

Parents may even have given up, thrown their adolescent away, either by having the kid locked up, or else by writing him or her off in their thoughts and emotions.

One thing is known: Any program for alcohol-abusing youths is more effective if parents are involved. Not only do parents need a place to vent their frustrations and compare notes with others in the same situation, but they must learn new tools to deal with their out-of-control youngster, to trade in the methods they used when the child was three or four years old.

The healing of an alcoholic family is slow, regardless of the problem. But it can, and does, happen. Things can get better.

To parents: It is my hope that this book can offer you some specific ways to cope with your alcoholic child, along with a deeper understanding of yourselves.

To young people who might be secretly concerned about what is happening to them as a result of drinking: There is a way out. It is not necessary to step off the curb into degradation and tragedy. And for you who may have stumbled, be assured that you *can* get up, dust yourself off and find a better way of living.

To anyone who can handle alcohol: If drinking is not consistently interfering in any area of your life, have at it. A relaxing drink or two at the end of the day, in shared conversation with friends or family, or enjoyed with meals, is what social drinking is all about.

This book is written to clear up existing myths about alcoholism, to state clearly the problem of teen and preteen alcohol abuse, to suggest methods for detection and interception of alcohol problems among youth (as young as seven years old), to assess creatively some of the obstacles that stand in the way of adult awareness of the problem.

The emphasis is how and where to go from here, from now —how to become "free from," to be "free to." It is not important that Mom may have kicked Junior's cat on a gray day in February five years earlier, which may or may not be the reason he has a drinking problem. The "why" shall be left to the psychiatrists and psychologists. In this book it will be enough to talk about how to recognize an alcohol-abusing youth and what to do about it.

My qualifications for writing this book are not academic. I gathered my own knowledge about alcoholism first-hand— while recovering from my own addictions. I am an alcoholic. I haven't used alcohol or any mood-altering chemicals for several years. My own experience and my contacts—as a counselor—with hundreds of adolescent and preadolescent abusers of alcohol and other drugs provide the basis for this book.

The cases I see are often tragic. But out of calamity is born humor. Learning to laugh at ourselves and with each other is the highest and most genuine form of therapy I know for alcoholics. It is impossible to laugh at problems and deny their existence at the same time.

One fifteen-year-old boy, a self-admitted alcoholic, told me how he had felt before and during the six years he had been problem drinking.

"For most of my life," he said, "I walked around waiting

for a spaceship to land, and a voice to say, 'Bill, it's time to go home now.'"

If nothing else, it is my sincere hope that this book will prove to kids like Bill, and their parents, that they are not alone. Nor are they wierd or alien because they couldn't predict the results of their drinking.

By facing honestly the fact that alcohol was wrecking their lives, and then doing something about it, they have become more creative, vital and happy human beings than they have ever been.

There is no spaceship coming to whisk them away, no other place where things will automatically get better for young alcoholics. Freedom comes only through dealing with the drinking problem. And "going home" is really just coming to know oneself.

2

Alcohol—the "Proper" Drug

"We are not moral men, we are businessmen." Mr. Bernbach of Doyle, Dane and Bernbach advertising agency on *The Today Show*, February 2, 1977. The liquor industry spends over 400 million dollars per year advertising their products.

☆   ☆   ☆

"The people are drinking more this year instead of smoking dope, and that's good for our business." Jim Monaghan, owner of a pub in the French Quarter of New Orleans, talking about the Mardi Gras.

☆   ☆   ☆

"I don't get loaded no more. My parents hassle me about pot. I just drink beer. They don't mind that." Bob, sixteen, has been arrested eight times for being drunk in public, drunk in an auto, possessing a dangerous drug (marijuana), drunk driving, and for burglary.

☆   ☆   ☆

Pat, fourteen, began coming to our group after drinking heavily for over two years. She had first suspected that something was wrong with the way she used alcohol after seeing a television movie about a teenage alcoholic girl.

Pat had suffered blackouts from the first time she drank, and while under the influence of alcohol had been sexually abused on two occasions—once by a neighbor boy and once by her father. Both Pat's parents are alcoholic.

Pat attended our group for four months. On nights the group met, she told her parents she was going to a friend's house to study. She had stopped drinking and using other drugs when her father beat her up.

Now, as the result of a court order, Pat is living with her grandparents in another city. She writes periodically, saying how much she enjoys the young people's AA group she attends.

☆   ☆   ☆

Young people, it appears, are moving away from hard drugs and toward alcohol. A turnabout has taken place. During the 1960s, parents used alcohol while their kids were into other drugs. Now the drugs have changed partners, and parents are getting stoned or loaded while the kids are getting drunk.

Check the facts. In 1974 there were over thirteen billion doses of amphetamines, barbiturates and tranquilizers produced in this country. THIRTEEN BILLION. While youngsters can—and do—get their hands on pills, for the most part Valium (mother's little helpers), Quaaludes, Seconals, Librium and the like remain in the private domain of the adult population. And that's a lot of pills!

At the same time, young people are continually being sold on the advantages of the drug, alcohol. One is hard pressed to turn on a television or radio, pick up a newspaper or magazine, or attend a gathering of any kind and not get a pitch to drink something spirited and fashionable. Alcohol users are portrayed as sexy, sophisticated, beautiful and successful. By the time a young person reaches eighteen years of age, he or she has watched, on the average, over 22,000 hours of television. That's equivalent to 550 forty-hour weeks or over ten years of employment for the average adult. And TV is only one of the media extolling alcohol as the "in" drug.

A ton of money is spent hawking booze—the Licensed Beverage Industry spends an estimated 400 million dollars yearly, in fact. All those millions have been earmarked specifically to get you and me to try Black Velvet on our friends, become breathless with Smirnoff's, come catch some well-dressed beauty with Kamchatka, or emulate the health and wholesomeness of the mountain man who drinks Hamm's Beer. Let's be honest. Distilleries and breweries and their advertising agencies push alcoholic beverages for one purpose, to get as many people as possible to drink their products. How liquor, beer or wine is used—by whom it is consumed—seems to be of token interest to them. Their aim is to persuade people, young and old, to use this addicting drug—the most abused drug in our society, and the one that is responsible for more deaths and carnage and human despair than any other.

To be sure, alcohol is the revered, "proper" drug of our culture. Where two or more are gathered, John Barleycorn will most likely be in attendance. On the movie screen, on television, at a neighborhood party, among a group of youngsters—booze is what is happening.

What are the reasons young people currently choose alcohol over other drugs? The most obvious answer is that it is easier to get. And the most popular place to score is home —either with parental permission or by stealing from the household liquor cabinet or from the frosted supply of beer in the refrigerator. Most adults keep alcohol around the house. Even those who do not drink often maintain a well-stocked bar to entertain friends who do.

As in Carla's case, mentioned earlier, children who sip away at their parents' liquor supply cover their trails in various and ingenious ways. One fifteen-year-old boy in our youth group siphoned off copious amonts from his father's private stock and replaced it with colored tea. The kid was cunning (as are most of those we see, bright ones using their creative energy in negative activities). He had left just enough alcohol in the bottles so they smelled like the real thing. He finally came under suspicion after his parents threw a party and their guests remained mysteriously sober. When his father found him drunk one afternoon, the kid boldly confessed his caper. The father was amazed to learn that his liquor had been pirated for over two years.

Many youngsters don't have to steal it; they are given a green light to drink at home, under their parents' watchful—and sometimes bloodshot—eyes. Adults rationalize this permissiveness by stating that they would rather have their children drink at home than on the street or playground.

All people adjust their preferences—about alcohol or anything else—according to their own experiences. But parents should at least be aware that by allowing, even encouraging, their children to drink at home, they are turning them on to a dangerous drug. So dangerous is it that alcoholism is ranked as the third leading killer in this country, after heart disease and cancer. Many experts contend that it would move up a notch or two on the list if more causes of death were labeled correctly. Doctors and coroners tend to protect surviving members of a family by writing something other than "acute alcoholism" on the death certificate. This practice may save embarrassment, but it also helps to further cloak the disease of alcoholism in the kind of stigma which has prevented many sufferers from admitting their problem. By thus implying that it is disgraceful to die of alcoholism, certain medical authorities have indicated that *having* the disease is also a disgrace. And people don't readily admit what they are ashamed of. Some would rather die first—and do.

How drinking at home affects a young person's attitude towards alcohol is largely unclear. But, as mentioned before, *the earlier a youngster begins drinking, the likelier it is that he or she will develop a drinking problem.*

The Orange County study of youth drinking patterns (offered in detail in Part Two) revealed that, of the eighteen-year-olds tested, forty-two percent qualify as problem drinkers or alcoholics. This means that twice as many young alcohol-users are problem-drinking as their adult male counterparts. Recent figures from northern California, Massachusetts, Maryland, New York, Colorado, Illinois and other states show almost identical results, indicating that the sharp rise in adolescent alcohol abuse is not limited to southern California.

Specifically, recent studies indicate that *the current crop of preteens and teens possess lower overall tolerance to alcohol than do the adult generations.*

Medical researchers currently are studying this phenomenon. Are youngsters less immune to alcoholism because of some genetic breakdown in tolerance to the drug? Does the same principle apply with sugar, since skyrocketing rates of diabetes and hypoglycemia (low blood sugar) might indicate that, as a society, we are less able to handle certain foodstuffs?

Until scientists resolve questions like these, it's best to stick with what we know. We *can* state, with evidence, the dimensions of adolescent alcohol abuse. And we *do* know the patterns an alcohol-abusing youngster follows. And we *can* predict that a high percentage of these early drinkers will develop problems with alcohol.

One of the difficulties in detecting a young person's drinking problem is that many times parents see only the consequences or resultant behavior of alcohol abuse—truancy, withdrawal from family affairs, stealing, fighting, loss of friends, trouble with the police. Because their children drink without their knowledge, most parents do not link this evidence with alcohol abuse. And not recognizing the root of the trouble, they may even attempt to get closer to the kid by encouraging him or her to drink with them at home. They go by the ill-conceived motto that "the family that tips booze together stays together."

In reality no one, including a parent, seems able to predict how any young person will handle alcohol.

Another favorite method youngsters use to obtain alcohol is to hit up a friend. The friend most likely has stolen it from *his* (or her) parents; the theft usually is undetected.

We live in an age of sociological change. Traditional family structure is shifting, and more and more children are living in homes either with a single working parent or with both parents employed. This makes for a great deal of unsupervised time in the house. Certain activities therefore can go on without parental knowledge or even suspicion. One of these is drinking. It has become increasingly easy for youngsters to gather after school at a friend's house, where no adult is present, and have a party. If kids are careful, these drinking sessions can take place over a period of years without detection.

Much has been written about "the criminal element" which lurks around school yards, turning kids on to drugs. With good reason, parents get up in arms, demanding that drug-pushers be prosecuted to the full extent of the law. Hard drugs are illegal and dangerous. *So is alcohol in the hands of minors.*

If you want to see the most common "drug-pusher" in our society, try this simple experiment: Park in front of a liquor store or supermarket around eight o'clock in the evening. Observe the number of minors, money in hand, who approach an adult to ask him or her to buy wine, beer or hard liquor. Kids call it "pimping some booze." Note the number of adults who do it. Don't be surprised if you see a fellow member of your PTA making the buy for the kids, the same father who screams about the ease with which "drugs" can be bought at school.

Even if a youngster is turned down a few times, he or she will invariably find someone willing to go in and buy the bottle or six-pack. In a pinch—and this is a scam I used to employ myself—the youngster can find a wino, or someone else who looks in need of a drink, and offer to share the booze if the older person will make the purchase. Very few people with a bad thirst will turn down such an offer.

Besides, any minor who wants alcohol desperately enough either has a false ID or a friend who can produce one. Highly profitable businesses exist for the primary purpose of manufacturing counterfeit identification for minors who want to buy alcohol. And only recently in some states have parents or other adults been prosecuted for willfully serving or procuring alcohol for a minor who subsequently gets into trouble with the law.

Another standby for thirsty youngsters is to find a "kegger" (several kids plan a party, buy the beer, hire a band and charge admission). Young people of all ages—no one checks ID cards at keggers—show up and drink until they pass out or the party is raided by the police, whichever happens first. These parties may draw upwards of 500 kids, some from as far away as fifty miles. For many of these, drinking beer is like throwing gasoline on a fire. Mornings following keggers, juvenile detention centers and county jails are packed with the ones who have been arrested for public drunkenness, disturbing the peace, open container, possession of alcohol, fighting or drunk driving—all waiting for their parents to bail them out.

Granted, then, alcohol is easy to come by for young people. But another reason for youth's shift in chemical preference is parental relief that Johnny or Mary is "only drinking" and not using other drugs, a kind of secondary approval, a backhanded sanction of alcohol.

Also, alcohol is inexpensive compared with other drugs. A lid of Colombian (good grade pot) is currently bringing 200 dollars on the street. You can buy a lot of hootch for 200 dollars. Young ones, looking to get loaded, try to get the most for their money—more bang for their buck, as the saying goes.

And the distillery companies, regardless of their slick public service advertisements imploring youth to drink intelligently and safely, have recognized this change in drug preference and cashed in. Pop wines and other drinks marketed specifically for youth have turned into a billion-dollar enterprise. Make no mistake about it, these products have been packaged, advertised and distributed solely for young people. (When was the last time you saw a business executive walk up to a bar and order a round of Strawberry Flings or Banana Kickers?) Pop wines may seem mild, but are just as potent as beer and most regular wines.

Why Youth Is Turning To Alcohol

In our society, drinking alcohol signifies the rite of passage from adolescence to adulthood. Using alcohol is coincident with being a grownup, whose rights and status a kid seeks. One way to declare adulthood is to drink alcohol—just like mom and dad.

Pressure from peers is undoubtedly one of the strongest influences on young people to drink. Most kids on the street today are drinking by age ten. The fact that "all the other kids do it" puts enormous pressure on a youngster, who is also going through the painful and awkward period of adolescence. During teen and preteen years, there is always a struggle for identity—a need to discover who and what you are—often by experimenting, by trying on several different roles. And of course this goes along with a powerful desire to be accepted by friends.

For any youngster today *not* to drink is difficult. An abstaining kid is labeled as strange or suspect, one who sells out or gives in to the adult community. In short, the young abstainer is alienated, a stranger among those whose approval he or she desperately seeks. Even for one who views drinking as a negative trip—maybe there is an alcoholic in the family—the mighty influence of friends makes it a lot easier to say yes than no when a drink is offered. Drinking makes an adolescent a member of the group, a part of something.

An inner pressure urging a youth to drink—one that has been inherent in the growing-up process since the beginning of time—is rebellion. Breaking laws of the "do as I say, not as I do" variety has always been a favorite pursuit of the young. And illegally drinking alcohol is considered fairly safe ground for "testing" and rebelling against the existing order.

Historically, courts have been overly lenient with adolescent alcohol abusers, even those who commit crimes while under the influence. Our justice system does not hold a minor accountable for his or her actions to the same degree as an adult. As we are a drinking society, juvenile justice authorities tend to treat adolescent alcohol abusers with patronizing permissiveness. It is somewhat hypocritical to come down hard on adolescents for doing what most adults in the probation office or court room probably do themselves with great regularity—drink alcohol. If that same juvenile were to get popped for LSD or a pocketful of pot, he or she would no doubt earn a harsher penalty.

It didn't take the youth of America long to figure out that using alcohol carries a much leaner sentence (if any) than using illicit drugs. In most states, cultivation of marijuana calls for a stiffer sentence than drunk driving. This is incredible when you consider that more than 30,000 people were killed on the highways last year as the direct result of drunk driving. (Statistics on "doped driving" are not available.)

Don't misunderstand. In no way do I advocate smoking pot, nor do I smoke it. It's just that, as a society, we need to review our crime and punishment precepts, as they apply to all drugs, and make the sentence fit the offense.

Any discussion of youth drinking patterns must take into careful consideration the times in which we live. Current conditions make growing up on the street ten or fifteen years ago seem like a piece of cake.

Today's preteens and teens are smarter and possess more street savvy than their predecessors. The youth of today has seen it all—including friends using hard drugs—has experimented with sex (what the rest of us used to fantasize about, they are now doing), participated in booze parties and observed murders, rapes and robberies regularly on television. During the 1950s "on the bricks," life moved at 33⅓ rpm; the 1960s saw it speed up to 45 rpm; and in the 1970s, a full-on 78 rpm and still whirling faster.

Our crop of adolescents are asked to handle situations and choose ways of living that could set the tone for their entire lives. They are offered alternatives that we who grew up yesterday only heard about. Using drugs is one of those choices, and with eighty-five percent of the kids drinking alcohol, at least occasionally, it is a small miracle when any youth selects abstinence over drinking.

There is tremendous pressure on any youngster to follow the crowd, lay down his or her principles and assume those of the peer group. The power of one's environment to govern personal choices has been well documented by social scientists.

The Family Development Program of Laguna Beach, California, a county counseling program working with families who have out-of-control minor dependents, uses as its motto: "If you don't believe in something, you'll fall for anything." Most young people don't know for certain what they believe in, if anything at all. Much of what they fall for is what their peers and adult models are doing. And what are those peers and adults doing? Drinking a lot of booze.

The federal government's massive antidrug campaign of the '60s and early '70s seems finally to be paying off and has been partially responsible for youth's choosing alcohol over other drugs. Untold funds have been spent on advertising which pointed out the dangers of hard drugs (much of this was based on hysteria and misinformation) and characterized anyone who used dope as a long-haired loser. Initially any drug the government campaigned against seemed to enjoy increased popularity—sort of a negative sanction—but the antidrug program at least has succeeded in crossing generational lines and promoting a kind of secondary boycott of illicit drugs.

The adolescents of today may have seen their older brothers and sisters do time for possession (in this country or abroad), turn into non-functioning vegetables or die from overdosing or eating or shooting bad drugs. These hard realities, even more than the government campaign against illicit drugs, seem to have gotten the point across. Although not all drug-users suffered any such fate, there were enough apparent dangers that went along with hard drugs—and strong questions about the effects of drugs bought on the street—to flash the warning to youth.

Certain high priests and priestesses of rock music and pop stars of television—always Sirens of influence on the young —died from hard-drug overdoses or took their own lives behind depressions accompanying chemical abuse. The list lengthened: Janis Joplin, Alan Wilson (Canned Heat), Jimi Hendrix, Lenny Bruce, Danny Whitten (Crazy Horse), Brian Jones (Rolling Stones), Tommy Bolin (Deep Purple), Freddie Prinze, Richard Peron—just some of the idols of the young whose deaths were linked with drugs.

Rock stars who survived heroin, cocaine and other drugs began warning of their perils through song lyrics. And some began espousing alcohol as the hip turn-on. Next to advice from friends, a young person will follow the recommendations of a favorite musician.

Singer Joe Cocker says, in an article in *Rolling Stone*, that he drinks "partly to forget everything—which is what booze is all about—and partly because I couldn't find anything decent to smoke in America." The unavailability of "anything decent to smoke," and the fact that Cocker had been busted for possession of heroin undoubtedly have been factors in his taking up the cause of alcohol.

Thus youngsters are getting the message that alcohol is safer and more acceptable to adult society and poses less danger to physical and mental health than illicit drugs. And isn't that what parents have been telling them all along? As kids swarm to alcohol, adults breathe secret sighs of relief. At least their children have agreed with them on *something*.

This adult acceptance of—even reverence for—alcohol and paranoia about illicit drugs has been reflected in government funding of alcohol education programs and treatment facilities for youth. Money earmarked specifically for treating the young alcoholic has been almost negligible until the middle '70s. In Orange County, for instance, the Department of Mental Health in 1977 budgeted 4.2 million dollars for treatment of "drug" abuse, while 1.2 million has been designated for programs for alcoholics of all ages. This ratio of funding is consistent with several metropolitan areas of the country. Until 1975 there were no programs in Orange County specifically for young alcoholics. Now there is one, privately funded, with a publicly funded program also being planned. There are over twenty programs for treatment of illicit drug abusers.

Drug enforcement officials are looking under the bed for illicit drugs while the kid is downing a bottle of booze in the kitchen.

Only a scattered few alcoholism treatment hospitals in the country have recognized the need for treatment of teen and preteen alcoholics and have set aside beds for that purpose. Even fewer have recruited alcoholism counselors who can offer the bridge of identification with adolescent patients.

In the Twin Cities of Minneapolis and St. Paul, Minnesota, several facilities treat alcoholics and other drug-abusers together effectively. The disease is chemical dependency, say many authorities in this field, whether the abused drug is alcohol, pot, LSD or other hallucinogens, heroin, cocaine, barbiturates, tranquilizers, glue, angel dust, over-the-counter or prescription pills of other kinds or what have you.

In other areas of the country where chemical dependency is not regarded as openly as in Minnesota, there is likely to be resistance to treating alcohol abusers together with other drug-dependent people—quite often on the part of the alcoholics, even though many youngsters are polydrug abusers.

Much of the responsibility for treatment of alcoholism has been left to Alcoholics Anonymous, the most successful treatment known. In fact, most programs that have proved to be effective are based on AA's principles, Steps and traditions. Although the situation is now changing, AA still is primarily a white, adult fellowship. AA meetings for and run by young alcoholics are scarce. Those tailored for children aged seven to thirteen are almost nonexistent. However, in forming special groups for minority groups, women, gay and non-smoking alcoholics, AA is exhibiting an anxious willingness to meet the needs of its new members.

To sum up what is happening on the streets: Although many continue to be hard drug and polydrug (mixing chemicals, as alcohol and pills) users, a solid majority of preteens and teens, over four to one, are choosing alcohol over other drugs. Government mental health departments and private abuse programs need to respond to this fact. Truth about alcohol and alcoholism must be delivered in a nonpreachy manner to school children as young as second or third graders, as well as to their parents and teachers, so that when these children do drink, the symptoms of abuse may be more quickly self-recognizable or detected by the adults around them. Or, even better, a youngster may then be better informed and able to make his or her own choice about whether or not to drink. He or she may even elect *not* to follow the urgings of drinking friends or the example of drinking parents.

For youngsters who are drinking out of control, effective detection and interception methods need to be further devised and standardized. Those working with kids (school counselors, psychologists, members of the clergy, parents and teachers) are often confused as to what constitutes alcohol abuse among young people; so much misinformation exists about what is or is not acceptable drinking behavior for teens and pre-teens. Most adults do not become aware of the problem until a youngster reaches late-early or middle stage alcoholism.

There is one quick and telling measure of what alcohol is doing to any young person's life: If drinking is interfering on a consistent basis with one or more areas of a youngster's life, he or she is most likely moving into alcoholism. More thorough measuring devices, including two questionnaires devised from the Orange County youth survey findings, are given in Chapter Eight.

3

Theories, Myths and a Few Facts

"We believe ... that the action of alcohol on these chronic alcoholics is a manifestation of an allergy; that the phenomenon of craving is limited to this class and never occurs in the average temperate drinker. These allergic types can *never**safely use alcohol in any form at all ..."
William Silkworth, M.D.

☆   ☆   ☆

"Alcoholism is a chronic disease, or disorder of behavior, characterized by the repeated drinking of alcoholic beverages to an extent that exceeds customary dietary use or ordinary compliance with the social drinking customs of the community, and which interferes with the drinker's health, interpersonal relations, or economic functioning."
Mark Keller,
Annals of American Academy of
Political and Social Scientists

---

*My emphasis.

☆   ☆   ☆

Belief in ". . . marijuana as the starting point in a career of drug use may well have been misplaced. First comes alcohol. If there is anything that comes before alcohol, it is hard to imagine what it might be . . . The first step may be mothers' milk."

Gould, Berberian, Kasl, Thompson and Kleber,
Sequential Patterns of Multiple-Drug Use Among High School Students.

☆   ☆   ☆

Jack, sixteen, had just passed the test for his driver's license three months before he came to our Youth Group. He had been using alcohol for three years, and other than not getting along well with his divorced mother, Jack seemed okay, handling school and holding down a part-time job.

One Saturday evening there was a dance at his high school, and he had permission from his mother to use her car. On the way to pick up his date, Jack stopped by a grocery store, and, with false ID, bought two six-packs of beer. He drank four cans before he arrived at the girl's house. She was sixteen. It was the first time they had gone out together. Enroute to the dance, Jack missed a turn in the road and flipped the car. He escaped with minor cuts and bruises. The girl was pronounced dead at the scene.

Jack attended our program for six months, along with some young people's AA meetings, both conditions of his probation. The accident had shocked him enough so that he stopped drinking for a time.

During one of our sessions, Jack shared with the group his sensations at the time of the accident. "The amazing thing was, the night it happened, I didn't feel drunk. I felt high, but in control. It was like the car was driving itself when it went off the road."

The last month we saw Jack, he told us he was doing a little drinking with friends. He didn't see any harm in having a beer or two, as long as he didn't try to drive after drinking. Jack felt he couldn't relate with friends at parties unless he drank.

Jack's mother and his father, an influential and wealthy Orange County attorney, liked the idea of our parents' group, but neither ever attended. They also said they did not object to their son's drinking, as long as he did it at home.

☆   ☆   ☆

There is a familiar cartoon depicting a pair of parents arriving home to find their daughter and her boy friend drunk and scantily clothed. The caption reads, "Thank God it's not pot."

Parents were terrified by the drug scare of the 1960s. They had good reason to be; youngsters by the thousands were turning on to illicit drugs. Young people strung out on heroin seemed to reinforce a widely held belief, that smoking pot was the first stop on the way to shooting smack. This was and is largely untrue. More heroin addicts start with the drug alcohol than any other.

Parents were relieved when sons or daughters were "only drinking." Adults understood alcohol, in most cases used it themselves, and were soothed by the realistic probability that their kids wouldn't get thrown in jail if they were caught drinking.

Along with nicotine and caffeine, alcohol is an accepted, respectable drug. It is sold over the counter, served to foreign dignitaries at state dinners, enjoyed in plushly decorated cocktail lounges and at family dinners. Among certain cultural groups it is considered a part of most meals. Alcohol for many is a relaxant, a pleasure to be shared with friends. The majority of drinkers are able to exercise restraint and self-control in using alcohol.

This is not true for addictive persons, those adults and young people for whom getting drunk or loaded becomes a way of life that is infinitely more important than NOT getting drunk or loaded. The addictive person differs from the nonaddictive one in the amounts consumed, the reasons for drinking and the consequences of his or her alcohol use. And one of those consequences is "getting hooked" psychologically and physically on the substance abused. The question—still unanswered—is whether the addictive person is destined to be hooked before he or she ever starts using chemicals or if it is the chemical itself that causes the addiction.

If our society had grasped the meaning of addiction and chemical dependency, we certainly would never have introduced "nonaddicting" heroin in the late nineteenth century as a cure for morphine addiction. Then, after thousands of people got hooked on heroin, "nonaddicting" methadone was pressed into action to withdraw these addicts from heroin. Now we have a whole new crop of addicts— methadone junkies. The word from the street is that government-supplied methadone, when combined with alcohol, provides a better high than the heroin it was intended to combat. And the beat goes on.

Addictive persons find it increasingly hard to leave chemicals alone once they start using them. Left to their own devices, they eventually require the chemical in order to function. Being high is the only way they can operate within a system that frightens and intimidates them.

Their lives begin to revolve around drinking or using other drugs—the parties they attend, the moods they try to change, the feelings they try not to feel. Job, school and home schedules are ruled by a secret and growing craving. Every relationship or situation in their lives takes a back seat to that craving.

In essence, an addictive person who uses mind-altering chemicals eventually must get hooked. The only variable is the amount of time it takes.

Addiction to alcohol, or other drugs, is progressive and is a disease. This is what one medical dictionary says about disease: "A definite morbid process having a characteristic train of symptoms . . . a process . . . cause may be unknown."

In the case of alcoholism, although the cause may still be unknown, the characteristic train of symptoms *is* known. And these can be recognized as alcoholism symptoms in young people and used for early interception of the disease.

Personality and biochemical differences between the addictive and nonaddictive person still are largely a mystery —as is why certain individuals, after appearing to drink normally and socially for years, slip into alcoholism.

What is known is that growing numbers among us seem to be incapable of using chemicals in a non-abusive fashion. As a young person in one of our groups said, "Anything I do twice I seem to get addicted to."

Addiction is not a respecter of social or economic levels. According to our Orange County youth drinking survey, socioeconomic status was completely unrelated to problem drinking.

The tendency to become addicted presents a puzzle so baffling that some of the finest scientific minds of our century, backed by millions of dollars, have been unable to solve it.

While many diverse descriptions of addiction have been published and discussed, whether someone inherits alcoholism, develops the disease or picks it up as a consequence of living in a certain environment still is under investigation— as it has been for decades.

Of course, there are theories. Theories about the causes of alcoholism are divided into two basic schools of thought, the social model and the medical model.

In the latter, research is attempting to establish what biochemical differences exist between the alcoholic and non-alcoholic person. Certain medical experts propose the X-factor theory, that some individuals are biochemically predisposed toward addiction. That is, a percentage of people are born with a kind of "pilot light," a factor that inclines them toward alcoholism. And a higher percentage of each succeeding generation, some researchers suggest, has little or no defense against chemicals—hence, the steady rise in the number of persons addicted to alcohol and other drugs.

The theory holds that if the person predisposed to addiction does not drink or use drugs, this inherent factor poses no threat to his or her physical, emotional and spiritual well-being.

But when those with the so-called X-factor or pilot light begin drinking alcohol, or using tranquilizers, barbiturates, amphetamines or narcotics, their pilot light ignites; certain electromagnetic and biochemical changes are set off in their systems.

Blood sugar imbalance also has been blamed for alcoholism. Do problem drinkers, for whatever reasons, have impaired sugar regulatory systems, making them more susceptible to inner cravings and depressions?

Or do alcoholics have neurochemical imbalances that predispose them toward addiction? Serotonin, a nerve transmitter chemical that aids in the function of brain cells (think of it as cerebral transmission fluid), has been thought to play an important role in determining whether a person drinks alcoholically or not. Too much serotonin, some say, spikes the individual's craving for alcohol. Lower the amount of serotonin, and the desire for the drug ebbs.

This waxing and waning seems to fit with the biorhythmists' theory that a craving for the relief of alcohol is heightened according to certain inner cycles.

Faulty metabolism, along with the alcoholic's purported inability to produce or assimilate certain vitamins essential to mental balance is another addiction-related tack being pursued by medical researchers. Lithium, an anti-depressant mineral, has been used in an attempt to flatten the curve of the alcoholic's violent mood swings and therefore lessen the desire to reach for a drink as an antidote to stress. Niacin,

Vitamin B and other agents are being used in experiments to try to right the alcoholic's supposed metabolic imbalance.

Also included in this medical model of alcoholism is the theory that the disease is inherited. That is, if one or both parents are alcoholic, their offspring run a greater than average risk of becoming alcoholics. Or, conversely, when there is no evidence of alcoholism in a family, the younger generation is less likely to be alcoholic. Except for a few benchmark statistics, studies conflict on these matters. The child of a parent who drinks alcoholically does stand a greater chance of becoming an alcoholic than one whose parents drink socially or are abstainers.

But there is also the fact that once children of abstaining parents begin drinking alcohol, they run a better than average chance of alcoholism. The number of young alcoholics from families where parents are social drinkers or abstainers is on the rise.

There are still many unanswered questions about the influence of heredity on alcoholism. For instance, more information needs to be gathered about the drinking patterns of children of alcoholic parents who stopped drinking before those children were old enough to remember what it was like to live in an alcoholic household.

Recent data, citing cases in which newborn infants of problem drinking mothers have suffered alcohol withdrawal symptoms (like convulsions) at birth could indicate that alcoholic toxicity is passed from one generation to the next.* Whether or not alcoholic toxicity at birth predisposes a child to the disease is still a matter of speculation.

Alcoholics Anonymous holds that when an alcoholic drinks, a physical allergy sets in, which is coupled with a mental obsession. The alcoholic then craves more to drink, and the allergic reaction is manifested in social and physical dysfunction.

---

*For more information on the effects on unborn babies of mothers' drinking during pregnancy, read Lucy Barry Robe's *Just So It's Healthy*, CompCare Publications, 1977.

The social model, called nurtured alcoholism, is based on the theory that a person becomes an alcoholic basically because of environment and what he or she is taught or not taught about drinking. Some social scientists lay the blame on feelings of guilt. No guilt, no alcoholism, they say. Others point to our social structure, which tolerates—even encourages—the consumption of alcohol. Drinking is a learned behavior, they state, and people use alcohol because their peers use it. Consuming large quantities of alcoholic beverages is regarded as a normal way to cope with the stresses and tensions of our high-pressure age. Proponents of nurtured alcoholism theories say some of these drinkers are bound to fall into alcoholic drinking.

Whatever the scientific reason, one thing appears certain. At some point in his or her drinking career, the addictive person begins using alcohol differently and suffers far more pronounced physical, emotional and social consequences than the nonaddictive person.

How do these theories apply to the youngest alcoholics?

The pilot light or X-factor theory seems especially relevant to younger people, many of whom are developing serious drinking problems after comparatively brief histories of using alcohol. The onset of the disease is often telescoped in adolescents.

From the social science point of view, there is no question but that powerful forces influence any youngster's behavior. How a young person dresses, talks, thinks and acts is largely dictated by surrounding conditions. (The fact that many parents dress and act like their adolescents points out the power of peer pressure—mighty enough to leap backwards from one generation to another.)

How any youth handles the painful, formative period of adolescence is highly dependent on family standards, peer influence and the prevailing culture of the young. Drinking patterns, claim some researchers, are formed during adolescence in a culture that espouses an outside-in formula for living, that looks for external cures for all problems and hurts and ills. "If something is bothering you," says this society, "or if you have a pain of any kind, reach for a chemical to take away the discomfort." Our dependence upon "taking something" to cure everything from a headache to depression, even to alter how we feel (or don't feel), is hardly surprising. A youngster hears advice of this kind from the time he or she is old enough to hold a thought—from radio and television (this pill for that ill or this brew for fun) as well as from the family doctor, parents and friends.

Whatever the reason—nature or nurture—alcoholism among youth is skyrocketing. Whether the disease is biochemical, hereditary or cultivated, one thing seems apparent: In this culture, our tolerance toward the drug alcohol seems to be dropping. The greater "immunity" to alcoholism seems to be eroding away with each succeeding generation. The percentage of alcoholics among this current crop of young people has been shown to surpass even the adult rate—by fifty percent in some areas of the country. And they are alcoholics before most of them are old enough to have a legal drink!

4

Who's Alcoholic?
Not Me. Not My Child.

"Alcohol is not my problem. If my parents and the cops would leave me along, I'd be all right," Drew, age sixteen, said after being sentenced to six months of alcoholism counseling, and two weeks before he was killed on his motorcycle. He was drunk at the time of the accident.

☆　☆　☆

"Therefore, it is not surprising that our drinking careers have been characterized by countless vain attempts to prove we could drink like other people. The idea that somehow, someday he will control and enjoy his drinking is the great obsession of every *abnormal** drinker. The persistence of this illusion is astonishing. Many pursue it to the gates of insanity or death." *Alcoholics Anonymous*, Second Edition.

---

*My emphasis.

☆   ☆   ☆

Don, eighteen, had become one of the top motorcycle racers on the West Coast. A handsome kid, he had a steady girl friend and had started to earn good money on the racing circuit. Several motorcycle manufacturing companies had offered him substantial fees to endorse their products. Don was flying high—too high.

Don had begun drinking every day and was doing cocaine to combat his depressions. He had started pulling no-shows at races, and when he did make it, he was generally too drunk to race. Track judges disqualified him from meets for being under the influence of alcohol.

Don decided he needed some time away. He and two friends went to Mexico for a week, so Don could "get his head straight." Their first day south of the border, after a heavy drinking session of "Tekillya Sunrises" (a popular drink among youth, consisting of tequila, orange juice and grenadine). Don rolled his car, and his two friends were killed.

After attending our group for three months, Don acknowledged that alcohol might be his problem, but felt he could safely smoke marijuana. The last I heard about him, he was living on a ranch for indigent alcoholic men. Don was not yet nineteen.

☆   ☆   ☆

"Alcoholism is a disease that tells people they don't have a disease." So goes one truism. And this denial is a major obstacle to recognizing, intercepting and interrupting the progress of the disease. It is also one reason why alcoholism is the third most common killer disease in this country. Young alcoholics are often snagged in a tangle of denial; they don't believe they have drinking problems, and neither do the adults around them.

At the present time, until an individual actually uses alcohol or mood-changing chemicals, it remains a mystery as to whether or not that person is addictive. Except for looking at the results—the consequences of drinking—there is no reliable test for alcoholism. And young drinkers are adept at hiding consequences from their elders, until those consequences become so flagrant they cannot be ignored.

Even then, youths who have caused family disruptions, who have been bounced out of school, arrested, placed on juvenile probation, treated by a physician or hospitalized— all because of abusing alcohol—still refuse to see drinking as their problem.

They are inclined to blame their alcohol-inspired troubles on parents, teachers, police authorities, probation officers and anyone else they can find as a scapegoat. Even those who have been arrested for drunk driving, in some cases more than once, hesitate to pin their problems on their drinking— an attitude that has spawned the saying, "Young alcoholics see things as they aren't."

Denial that alcohol is at the center of a young drinker's difficulties can be illustrated by the results of our recent study in Orange County (see Part Two).

Let's look at blackouts—one of the main indicators of alcohol abuse—a condition caused by overdosing with alcohol (a central nervous system depressant) until that part of the brain that governs memory is put to sleep. Someone in an alcoholic blackout continues to function, sometimes destructively, but simply doesn't remember what went on during the time of impaired memory. The blackout is the infant of the "wet brain," which occurs when someone drinks enough alcohol over a sufficient period of time to render their brain incapable of remembering simple things like how to eat or how to take off one's pants to urinate.

Of the 2,500 youngsters we questioned, twenty-four percent indicated that they blacked out from drinking, a red flag of early-stage alcoholism. *On the other hand, only two percent of those polled admitted they might have a drinking problem.* Inconsistent as it may seem, thirteen percent did admit that alcohol had caused them trouble at home and in the community, and seven percent had been arrested because of drinking. This disparity between blackout drinking (reality) and denial of the drinking problem (how the drinker sees reality) points out another difference in point of view: How a young person defines alcohol abuse may be totally inconsistent with society's or the medical community's definition. Misinformation about alcohol, combined with the nature of the disease itself, makes denial of its misuse particularly common among youth.

Immaturity demands instant gratification, high feelings, here and now. For a young person, the experience of drinking alcohol fills that bill, at least temporarily. Alcohol offers an escape from boredom, social inadequacies, an unhappy home life, and a solution to any other problem of growing up on this planet. For an increasing number, the solution has become the problem. The adolescents' vehicle of escape from the pains of growing up has turned on them, revoking liberties and blocking the maturing process.

Don't be misled, especially if you have an alcohol-abusing child in your home. In spite of appearances to the contrary, he or she does not really want the heartache, anxiety, restrictions, fines, probation status and general lack of control that come with abusing alcohol. No one chooses the misery that accompanies out-of-control drinking. No one plans to be arrested for drunk driving, smash up the family sedan or get thrown out of school. A person doesn't elect to become an alcoholic; it just happens. The young alcoholic temporarily loses the power of choice, and no number of warnings about controlling or cutting down on the drinking works.

The first step toward overcoming the problem is to help tear down the young alcoholic's denial mechanism, to attempt to intercept and alter his or her destructive course of alcohol abuse. Often this means listening to what is *not* being said, hearing the appeal for help behind all the bluster, grandiosity, excuse-making and delusion of denial.

Parental denial of a child's drinking problem, even when the youth's alcohol abuse is causing out-and-out trouble in school or elsewhere, also can delay or prevent recognition of the real problem. Many parents, through lack of awareness or fear of the stigma attached to alcoholism, postpone admitting that their child's drinking has gotten out of hand. Other parents simply refuse to believe the obvious because it seems to point to their failure as parents. Parents should understand that a child's drinking patterns and their effectiveness as parents are, in most cases, unrelated. The child is drinking because he or she feels it is "getting the job done" (allowing the young person to continue the drinking behavior without really feeling the resulting guilt or discomforts).

Of course, if a parent of a drinking child also abuses alcohol, he or she is doubly unwilling to call a problem-drinking youngster's trouble by its right name. By even hinting that the child might be alcoholic, a mother or father could be forced to analyze her or his *own* drinking patterns. (Of the youths polled in our survey, more than a third— thirty-six percent—claimed that one or both of their parents were daily drinkers.)

When both parent and child have a drinking problem, this creates a double-blind concept of reality. The parent's refusal to recognize the child's drinking as out of control is only part of the delusion. The adult's abnormal drinking pattern has been set as a model for the child, thereby fogging that young person's ability to recognize that his or her own alcohol consumption and its consequences are at a problem level. Destructive dynamics of two-way denial and negative comparison block detection and treatment of alcoholism within such a family.

The problem-drinking parent becomes increasingly frustrated over the youngster's behavior, but is unable to pin it on drinking, lest the veil of denial be lifted from his or her own drinking. This sets the stage for more drinking by the parent, which creates more tension in the home, which gives the child more impetus to drink in order to blot out the unhappiness in the household. Both parent and child blame the situation on each other—and keep on drinking.

Teachers also may deny problem drinking among their students unless they have been trained to recognize certain symptoms. To illustrate this point: Recently I was scheduled to speak to a fourth grade class at nine in the morning. The talk had been arranged by the school nurse as part of a three-day alcoholism awareness program for grades four through seven. The teacher questioned the purpose of my talking to fourth graders about alcohol abuse. As part of my presentation, I asked the children to answer anonymously twenty questions related to their drinking habits.

The result? Four of the forty students had already suffered tangible consequences of alcohol abuse. They had either missed school because of drinking; stolen money to buy beer, wine or liquor; gone without lunch and spent the money on booze; raided their parents' liquor supply; or been treated by a physician for alcohol-related injuries. And I privately related to the teacher that I had smelled alcohol on two of the kids, eight and nine years old, who obviously had been drinking in the morning before school.

The school was located in an upper-middle-class area where prospective buyers must enter a lottery for the "privilege" of purchasing a house.

The teacher was mortified and has since enrolled in an evening alcohol education course in order to be better equipped to handle such problems in her classroom.

In defense of grade school and high school teachers, many have their hands full just covering course material. In schools where budgets have been cut and teachers' responsibilities increased, detection of alcohol-abusing students and their referrals into appropriate treatment become an added burden for the instructor. But whether teachers or special chemical dependency counselors cope with the problem, schools do need a built-in problem-drinking detection system to link with appropriate helping agencies in the community.

Teachers themselves (between ten and fifteen percent,

depending on whose statistics you believe) have problems with alcohol. Like the alcoholic parent, a problem-drinking educator denies it, and thus chooses, consciously or unconsciously, not to recognize alcohol problems among the students. If these teachers can call a kid's problem something other than alcoholism, they can diagnose their own drinking problems as something else, too.

The problem-drinking denial syndrome is, of course, not limited to teachers. It can be found also among school nurses, psychologists and administrators, prompting them to deal with the symptoms of a student's alcohol abuse rather than the problem itself — drinking.

Many educators and school administrators simply do not believe the problem of youth alcoholism to be serious. They are sometimes blocked from investigating the extent of kids' drinking by school district officials, mostly noneducators who do not deal directly with youth. Of the first sixteen schools we had designated to study in our Orange County youth drinking survey, twelve refused us entrance. Most of the resistance came from school board officials. Reasons given for their refusals ranged from "disruption of school schedules" to no reason at all. One school board member said, "If it came out that there is a problem with alcohol among the school children of this district, we would have a bad time selling houses here." He owned a major real estate firm in the area.

Some school officials and personnel blindfold themselves to youth drinking because, as one general counselor put it, "We open up a can of worms—and then what do we do about it once we recognize the problem?"

The "what do we do about it?" question often is left hanging because of divided responsibility for initiating alcoholism programs in the schools. Is it the responsibility of the individual school districts? Or of the local mental health boards or other county agencies? In our case, we had been hired by the Orange County Board of Supervisors to conduct the youth drinking survey. The testing program had been approved by the departments of mental health and education, who have little or no authority over individual school districts, although they have been charged with providing abuse programs.

Until such time as state, county and district agencies can agree on how to proceed, the battle against youth alcohol abuse will remain hit-and-miss.

Denial of youth alcoholism is apparent even in our justice system. Juvenile justice authorities and law enforcement officials often are reluctant to label alcohol-abusing youngsters as such. This is rather incredible when one considers that between eighty and ninety percent of those locked up in penal institutions are there as a direct result of abusing alcohol or other drugs. Our legal system is based on the promise that each individual will have the privilege of suffering or enjoying the consequences of his or her actions. Young people who break the law need to have the opportunity to face the consequences, to clean up their own messes; otherwise the law means nothing.

It is estimated that more than seventy-five percent of those released from prison are not rehabilitated and are destined to return there. Closer analysis by juvenile justice officials of an arrested youth's drinking or other drug-taking, along with good alcoholism treatment programs within closed-care facilities, might reduce markedly the rate of juvenile recidivism.

Denial of the widespread sickness of alcoholism—by individuals who suffer from it, by those close to them and by a society which religiously protects the traditionally accepted uses of the drug—is a primary reason why programs for problem-drinking youth have been slow to be initiated. Denial exists at all levels, among all ages. Until we are willing to look for the real villain—alcohol abuse—behind a high percentage of crime, truancy, violence, vandalism, general social upheavals and physical and mental ills, we are shutting out reality and denying ourselves the possibility of dealing with the problem.

5

Young, Female and Alcoholic

"We are children of our landscape; it dictates behavior and even thought in the measure to which we are responsive to it."

Lawrence Durrell, *Justine*.

☆   ☆   ☆

"But she was only drinking. You'd think she was using drugs or something." The mother of a twelve-year-old girl who had been suspended from school for drinking between classes.

☆   ☆   ☆

Jana

Jana, at fourteen, had run away from home twice. Each time, after being caught, she was placed in Juvenile Hall. There were two other arrests for open container (of beer). And she had been suspended from school three times for drinking.

Jana admitted that she had been drinking since the age of nine. Her main supply of alcohol came from her parents' liquor cabinet, a fact they had discovered only recently.

Twice she had been caught breaking into neighboring houses and stealing bottles of liquor, but was never prosecuted. Both times her parents paid the neighbors for their loss.

Jana's parents had heard about our program at a school PTA meeting and began attending our parents' group, where they hoped to learn some new ways of dealing with their daughter and her drinking problem. They made it a condition of Jana's probation that she attend our youth group.

That was a year ago. Jana has come every Wednesday, and nine months ago joined Alcoholics Anonymous. She has been free from alcohol and other drugs for five months. She is back in school, and her behavior at home has improved.

Jana, and others like her, have played an important role in our youth group. They offer a different kind of peer pressure to other youngsters—a positive kind full of hope that says, by example, that a kid can make it without getting drunk or loaded. Jana proves to the others that a youngster can clean up her life and make some healthy decisions about herself. She demonstrates an essential principle: You can learn to walk through life's ups and downs without taking uppers and downers.

Her parents offer a separate example to *their* peers. By regaining control of their household and unlocking themselves from Jana's poor behavior, they have become a model for other parents in the same situation. They have shown newer members of our parents' group that they are not alone, that there is a way out.

Jana has also received some unexpected fringe benefits of sobriety. Two of her classmates have approached her for help with their drinking problems. Liking what they saw in Jana, Sara and Debbie became members of our group and also joined AA. Jana's changes had appealed to them. Examples like Jana's are—and always have been—the greatest promotion for any way of life.

A kind of protective prejudice exists in our adult society which hushes up, in a sort of women-aren't-supposed-to-act-like-this embarrassment, the problems of the young female alcoholic. Of the one thousand or so youngsters we have seen in the youth program of the Alcoholism Council of Orange County, only five to ten percent were girls. These girls have been referred to us by juvenile probation or the courts after having been arrested for abusing alcohol, some several times. The small percentage might indicate that young females have less difficulty with alcohol, or even drink less frequently, than their male counterparts.

Our study exposed this idea as pure myth.

Young males and females showed only slight differences in per capita consumption of alcohol, a disparity largely explained by the fact that boys, on the average, weigh more than girls. Since body weight is a determinant of how much alcohol the system can assimilate, boys tend to drink slightly more than girls.

Amount of consumption is not necessarily a predictor of problem drinking. Amounts of alcohol that might prove troublesome to one person are of less significance to another. Alcohol affects people differently depending on several factors, like body weight, whether a person eats before drinking, general physical health and predisposition to addiction (that mysterious undefined factor). It is what alcohol *does* to the young person that indicates whether or not he or she is a problem drinker.

In terms of pathological predictors in our study (drinking alone, drinking to feel more at ease with oneself or others, drinking to combat depression, blackout drinking) teen and preteen females scored just as high as males. *Though females consume slightly less in quantity, there is virtually no difference between young females and males in consequences and pathology resulting from abusing alcohol.*

There is, however, a solid difference in how problem drinking is detected and diagnosed in young females and in young males. Though girls have as much trouble with their drinking as boys, there appears to be a reluctance on the part of adult society—especially juvenile justice authorities and parents—to recognize drinking problems in young females.

45

Of course, in our macho culture, drinking and getting into trouble are things boys do!

Because of this kind of stereotyped expectation, a great deal of societal stigma is attached to a young female's admitting she has a drinking problem. When a girl finally does make it to our program, she has been arrested more times, on the average, than the boys we see.

Many parents of young female alcohol abusers we have talked with admit they have looked the other way, refusing to acknowledge the signs of problem drinking in their daughters. Fear that a daughter may be stealing, sleeping around or suffering from a sullied reputation are the most frequently mentioned reasons for parents protecting a girl— and themselves—from the truth about her drinking.

Even when a daughter's drinking brings police trouble, these parents label her entanglements as behavioral or peer-influenced ("It's those friends she runs around with!") rather than alcohol-related.

Only when evidence becomes undeniable do most parents seek help for their daughters.

For some reason, juvenile justice authorities and mental health workers often project the same denial as parents. Not until most other rationales for the teen or preteen girl's poor behavior have been given and other forms of treatment attempted do these adults link her difficulties with her consumption of alcohol.

Recent findings indicate that valuable time and funds— and lives—could be saved if a female's drinking habits were the *first* determinant in diagnosing her dysfunction.

A young alcohol abuser is a young alcohol abuser, regardless of the individual's sex. If a girl is showing symptoms of alcoholism, she needs help. Alcoholism, in either males or females, doesn't go away by hoping or ignoring the signs. The sooner a child or adolescent is given information about alcoholism and tools for dealing with it, the greater the chance for recovery. Waiting only makes the wreckage more widespread and draws the net of addiction tighter.

6

Education and Prevention:
What Do They Really Mean?

"Further sluggishness in pulling this illness (alcoholism) out from under the rug would only add to the already unconscionable delay in addressing the scientific community to this overwhelming problem.

"Fortunately, the responsible medical community has seen fit to meet this challenge with honesty and candor. The American Medical Association, American Psychiatric Association, American Public Health Association, American Hospital Association, American Psychological Association, National Association of Social Workers, World Health Organization, and the American College of Physicians have now each and all officially pronounced alcoholism as a disease. The rest of us can do no less."

Stanley E. Gitlow, M.D.
Alcoholism: A Disease.

☆   ☆   ☆

Bob, sixteen, offered this explanation to our group one night. "I started drinking in the sixth grade. I would come home from school, and my older brother would have friends over. They liked to get me drunk, so they could trip out on me."

"They held you down and made you drink?"

Bob smiled. "Well, they used to offer it to me." He had been a blackout drinker since the age of twelve.

☆   ☆   ☆

If you want to give an adolescent a case of the yawns, show him or her one of the films made during the 1960s about alcoholism. A sampling of those cinematic arguments against alcohol abuse features gory scenes of fatal accident victims being pried from crumpled vehicles on freeways; a trembling fifty-five-year old wino being arrested for the thirtieth time that year (and the calendar in the police station announces that it's only August); an alcoholic housewife waking up in the company of a man she met in a bar and trying to shovel him out of the house before the kids wake up.

Or how about one of the medical flicks, starring close-up shots of diseased livers, hearts and brains in full color, demonstrating the effects of thirty years of hard drinking.

These themes are true. And these situations do happen. But most of them have little relevance for a thirteen-year-old with or without a drinking problem. Young people turn off to a "preachy" approach to alcohol abuse. If the danger is not clear and present, if the problem is not recognizable from their points of reference, if it is not presented in their own language, they do not identify with the message. Youth is, as we all know, inclined to live in the here and now.

Any educational methods that move the young drinker to anxiety and guilt don't necessarily help him or her get on top of the drinking problem. In fact, these feelings can have the opposite effect, adding fertilizer to an already overgrown sense of self-pity and therefore providing an excuse to drink more.

Most alcohol-abusing kids drink for the effects and are simply not intimidated by what might or might not happen to them twenty years hence. It makes no sense to expect them to identify with a film about the physical, emotional or moral manifestations of long years of hard drinking. This is as logical as expecting an adolescent to react to the antismoking campaign in which a middle-aged movie star appears on TV and announces that he has quit smoking, apparently with as much inner turmoil as deciding to brush his teeth. To that kind of "education," a young person will retort, "When I get to be his age, I'll quit, too."

Unfortunately if you're addicted to either nicotine or alcohol, ridding yourself of your habit is not quite that easy. And many young alcoholics don't make it to middle age; if they put off making the choice, they may have no choice at all.

One of the first jobs of an alcohol education program is to dispel some of the myths about alcoholism. Let me offer an example. When speaking in grade schools, I ask the kids to help me "build" an alcoholic. I pose a series of questions on who is most likely to be an alcoholic. Invariably we end up with the following description:

Sex: Male

Age: In his fifties.

Physical description: Red-faced, hair slicked with sweat, unshaven, sloppy about habits and personal appearance.

Clothes: World War II overcoat, Salvation Army wardrobe.

Job: None.

Place of residence: Doorway, washing machine shipping crate or Goodwill pick-up box in the inner city.

Married: No.

Education: Little, possibly eighth grade.

The kids are astonished to learn that the alcoholic they have "built" as typical is one that represents about three percent of the alcoholic population of this country. Generation after generation of children have been taught this myth by their parents, friends, teachers and by stereotypes in film, television and print. A respectable person with a drinking problem may be regarded as entertaining; the skid row bum is looked upon as pitiable. Certain comedians have made their living impersonating lovable, laughable and socially tolerated drunks.

Along with our misconceptions about the "typical" alcoholic comes the denial of the disease—both by those who have it and by those who refuse to recognize it in others. If you don't look and act like the person described above, you can't be an alcoholic!

When questioned about his or her drinking habits, a person tends to call upon this hidden image of the wino and secretly affirm, "That's an alcoholic. I might drink a little too much, but I'm not like that. If I ever get that bad, I'll quit." Unfortunately, for most, the mind or the body gives out, or they attempt to redecorate another automobile or a freeway bridge, before they "get that bad."

The most effective youth education programs use straight talk and non-scare tactics. They pose medical and social facts about alcoholism in an unpatronizing way, in terms a youngster can understand. (Kids always have their own kind of talk, and adult jargon can be like a foreign language to them.)

When presenting information about alcohol, it is equally important to point out what constitutes social drinking, thus setting a standard of accepted alcohol use.

Also, attractive alternatives to drinking need to be presented, along with tools to improve life.

The best that educators can hope for, in a general alcohol education program, is that the ones who *don't* have a drinking problem will get the message. Those who do have alcohol problems are inclined to turn off educational material on the topic. In our Orange County study, eighteen percent of the students claimed to shut off their ears when their teachers broached the subject or someone came to their school to talk about it. Again, that is part of the armor called denial.

It's not that the addictive youngster is not able or smart enough to absorb facts about alcohol abuse. Of the 1,000 or so young problem drinkers we've seen in our program at the Orange County Alcoholism Council, most are really bright kids. If it were a question of knowledge or learning ability, there would not be the alcoholism problem in our society today. But much more than intelligence is involved. For the addictive person, drinking has simply become more important than *not* drinking, and will continue to be so until he or she is no longer protected from the consequences of drinking behavior.

An alcoholic kid will view any education about alcohol as boring and irrelevant unless it applies to his or her own specific drinking problem and shows how it interferes with his or her own life. Until the young alcoholic learns to live in this world chemically free, no amount of education is going to be a preventive to abusing alcohol.

A young drinker's dilemma is just as baffling as any adult alcoholic's. Although every indicator says that alcohol is costing everything he or she values, the alcoholic continues to drink.

Alcoholic individuals would love to be able to drink socially, to enjoy the effects of the alcohol they crave without the accompanying hassles. The idea that somehow this might be possible keeps them drinking. In the face of all the hard-to-refute evidence, their drinking has reached alcoholic proportions, and there is no way to return to social drinking.

"I can quit anytime I want to," says the alcoholic, only to try it and find it can't be done. The craving for alcohol and the relief it offers makes shreds of promises he or she has made to self, parent, friend, family member, judge, proba-tion officer, spiritual adviser, employer or whomever else. Alcoholics have a way of forgetting all promises once they begin drinking.

No real evidence proves that educating youngsters about the medical and sociological consequences of problem drinking will prevent them from abusing alcohol. However, lectures on the effects of alcohol on the pancreas, liver, heart, stomach, bank account, job, nerves, brain, family and quality of life *may* have a certain value to youth in retrospect. The information *may* get filed away for future reference and hasten their recognition of their own drinking problems. But in no way has it been shown to *prevent* alcoholism. An individual whose drinking is already in the problem zone needs treatment, and until his or her drinking has been isolated by its consequences—specific consequences in his or her own life—general knowledge of the disease and how it affects others means very little.

A kid who wants to get high wants to get high *right now*. A malfunctioning liver or pancreas or heart can be taken into account later—much later. A young person sees his physical being as invulnerable; good health is guaranteed, a birthright.

And for those alcoholic adolescents caught in a don't-care-what-happens-to-me pattern of self-destruction (whether it is real or an attention-getter), abusing their health through overuse of alcohol is just part of that same pattern. More is required than just a few warnings about health to reverse a poor self-image.

In planning alcohol awareness programs for schools, special consideration should be given, therefore, to the age of the children and their ethnic backgrounds. In San Diego, California, a local chapter of the National Council on Alcoholism sponsors a puppet show to present facts about alcohol and alcohol abuse to elementary school in a non-preachy and humorous manner.

In areas with heavy Chicano populations, Hispanic programs are presented. Chicanos, who have a high rate of alcoholism in this country, view hard drinking as "machismo," upholding traditions of rugged manhood and masculine superiority over the environment. And alcohol is considered part of that environment. New programs for Spanish-speaking communities attempt to show that alcoholism detracts from the macho image, that the disease brings loss of self-respect and freedom, and that, for the alcoholic, sobriety means strength and freedom.

Children from a certain cultural background obviously relate better to a speaker on alcoholism if that person shares a similar origin. In many urban areas of the country, Spanish-speaking and Black alcoholism associations have speaker resources to serve schools where they are most needed. Alcoholics Anonymous, in sending speakers into schools, is sensitive to this need and tries to assign recovered alcoholics of appropriate ages and backgrounds to share their experiences at schools with high percentages of Hispanic, Native American, Black or Oriental students. (There are now several specific non-drinking social clubs for ethnic minorities in many neighborhoods across the United States.)

A kind of alcohol education which appears to have little effect as a deterrent to alcohol abuse is teaching youngsters to "drink properly," sip instead of gulp, never drink on an empty stomach, mix hard liquor with plenty of water or soda, pace themselves when drinking. Again, this type of information might make sense to those who don't have a drinking problem. Those who do, since they drink mostly to feel the effects, are not interested in methods of drinking that might deter or postpone those effects. Young people who are prone to addiction probably could not follow such a manual on social drinking anyway. They are the ones with the pilot light, the inner craving. Attempting to teach an addictive youngster how to drink normally is like trying to explain motherhood to a bull.

Alcohol is the agent that satisfies the alcoholic's deep thirst and offers him or her chemical release from psychic pain. But the young alcohol abuser must deal ultimately with her or his inner person and whatever it is that seeks relief through the drug, alcohol.

53

Proponents of teaching young people how to drink moderately cannot produce any hard facts to back them up. Instead, recent studies show that to teach a preteen to drink alcohol is to increase substantially that youngster's chances of developing serious problems with alcohol. In areas where the legal age to purchase and drink alcohol has been lowered, the alcoholism rate has continued to increase dramatically among youth, strongly indicating that learning "how to drink" at an earlier age is no deterrent to adolescent alcoholism.

Those that espouse teaching youngsters to drink and removing laws against minors purchasing alcoholic beverages should take note: Many youngsters begin abusing alcohol before they are in their teens, and by relaxing or removing age laws governing the use of the drug by youth, we also release alcohol-abusing youths from the legal consequences of their drinking. This actually promotes more problem drinking, since it postpones the day when a young person must fact his or her out-of-control drinking. The young drinker's alcohol-induced havoc goes unchecked.

Alcoholism prevention, as we know it, has not worked. When it comes to a pill, vitamin, therapy model or other panacea to avoid contracting the disease, science is basically where it was when humans first started crushing and fermenting grapes. Nor can education be counted upon to actually *prevent* alcoholism.

This is not to say that the search for an alcoholism preventive should not be continued. Anything that might relieve the massive suffering caused by alcoholism needs to be explored to the limit.

But if, as many say, "there is no such thing as prevention of alcoholism," we need to review the semantics which relate to drinking behavior. *Prevention of alcoholism may come to be known as prevention of some of its later and more serious consequences.* Some call this "early intervention."

Until a young person exhibits early stage indicators of alcoholism, he or she is not a problem drinker. The earlier the diagnosis of potential problem drinkers among preteens can be made, the more possible it may be to prevent the consequences of alcohol abuse.

Prevention, then, can be construed as avoiding as many of the miseries of alcoholism as possible, through the implementation of the earliest possible warning devices of problem drinking, and providing effective treatment modalities for preteens and teens.

How can we pinpoint the potential problem drinkers—as well as the ones who are showing early signs of problem drinking? Is there a way to standardize the definition of youth alcohol abuse and the tests for symptomatic indicators of early stage alcoholism? We have put together some tests for young people based on the information gathered in our Orange County survey as well as on national testing standards for detecting alcoholism among youth. Details are given in Chapter Eight.

7

An Ounce of Prevention?
Not in Daddy's or Mommy's Drink!

"Alcoholism is an illness characterized by preoccupation with alcohol and loss of control over its consumption, such as to lead, usually, to intoxication if drinking is begun; by chronicity; by progression; and by tendency towards relapse. It is typically associated with physical disability and impaired emotional, occupational and/or social adjustments, as a direct consequence of persistent and excessive use of alcohol."

> The American Medical Association,
> *Manual on Alcoholism.*

☆   ☆   ☆

"But the actual or potential alcoholic, with hardly an exception, WILL BE ABSOLUTELY UNABLE TO STOP DRINKING ON THE BASIS OF SELF-KNOWLEDGE."*

> *Alcoholics Anonymous*, Second Edition.

---

*My emphasis.

☆　☆　☆

Bobby

Bobby, age eight, was brought to our group by his mother. She had discovered him drunk on several occasions, and one of her neighbors had filed a complaint with the police that Bobby had broken into her house and stolen some valuables.

In the initial interview, Bobby's mother had said, "I'm not against his drinking. I gave him his first one six months ago with dinner. I let his two brothers drink beer around the house, but they don't act like he does."

Bobby later admitted to keeping alcohol in his school locker. He drank every day and spent whatever money he could get his hands on to buy booze. His money came from pilfering from his mother's purse and stealing from people in the neighborhood. Bobby had broken into houses more than twenty times in the previous three months. When he couldn't get alcohol or the money to buy it, Bobby stole tranquilizers from his mother's medicine cabinet. She had been a heavy Valium user for five years.

During a recent talk at Juvenile Hall, I noticed Bobby in the audience. He had been sent there for stealing a bottle of liquor from a supermarket and was slated to spend his tenth birthday in the hall.

☆　☆　☆

Parents have gone to some lengths to protect their children from alcohol and other drugs. They have tried to oversee their friendships, kept them away from places that serve alcohol, steered them into extra-curricular sports, even moved out of the city to a farm or a small town in hopes of avoiding the chemical scene.

None of these methods are foolproof. Old reliable friends who were childhood playmates become, almost overnight, drinking buddies. Participation in sports is no armor against alcohol abuse. And a small-town or country school is just as likely to be full of young drinkers as an urban one.

Can you protect a child from becoming an alcoholic? As long as our society is alcohol-dependent and espouses the outside-in recipe for satisfaction, as long as drinking alcohol has become part of every facet of living—from business to pleasure—the answer is, "Probably not."

One school of thought about how to deter problem drinking among youth is for parents to remove the mystique and guilt from drinking and teach their offspring to drink intelligently.

Generations of parents have tried conscientiously to do this. And this theory of exposing a child to alcohol early, thus satisfying childish curiosity, has been shared by many high-ranking authorities in the alcoholism field, including Dr. Morris Chafetz, former head of the National Institute on Alcohol Abuse and Alcoholism (NIAAA). He has stated publicly that teaching a youngster to sip, rather than gulp, alcohol, and allowing him or her to drink at home, would reduce his or her chances of becoming an alcoholic.

In their book, *Why Our Children Drink*, Edward and Jovita Addeo outline methods of instructing youngsters on how to drink alcohol so they will not develop a problem later in life. For instance, let them, they say, sample your drinks when they ask.

The "drink responsibly" theory has gotten attention from the press, been the subject of advertisements by the liquor industry and of dangerously generalized and misleading studies such as the controversial Rand Report of 1976. The "drink responsibly" campaign recently has been abandoned by the NIAAA, as its new director, Dr. Ernest Noble, saw the concept as counter-productive to the field of alcoholism treatment. Or more simply, it hasn't worked.

Noble and others believe the "drink responsibly" campaign may be effective, but *only for the non-addictive person.* Those predisposed to alcoholism, the pilot-light people, are simply unable to use the drug responsibly for any length of time. Intellectually they may understand how to drink socially, and even do so for certain periods. Over the long haul, they cannot maintain a pace of social drinking without going over the line into alcoholism. For the addictive person, alcohol is too often the solution which satisfies an inner craving, a hidden obsession the non-addictive person does not have. When a pilot-light person drinks, alcohol keeps on gaining in importance, to the point where inner standards of drinking are submerged or rationalized away.

The situation is no different for a young person who is addictive. Predisposition to alcoholism is predisposition to alcoholism; age doesn't matter. Or, as the sober young ones in our group say, "The square root of crap is still crap."

Alcohol is an addictive drug and the manner or place in which it is consumed has little bearing on the kid's resultant drinking pattern. From our Orange County survey, fifty-seven percent of the youngsters who drink got their first drink at home from their parents. And an alarming number of these kids (up to forty-two percent) already are drinking out of control. As stated before, *research shows that the earlier a youngster starts drinking, the greater the chance he or she will become an alcoholic. Where* a youth gets alcohol is not so much a determining factor of alcoholism as *when* he or she gets it. There appears to be no way the addictive person can drink safely, regardless of whether that person begins drinking at home at the knee of a parent or sneaks a drink from a friend's bottle on the school playground.

A home instruction course in safe drinking makes as much sense as teaching your child to skin-pop heroin (the method of injecting heroin into the fatty tissue, rather than directly into the vein) in hopes that the youngster will not become addicted. No one—from parents to some of the finest scientific researchers in the world—has been able to pinpoint the exact cause of addiction or identify who might be predisposed to alcoholism. Teaching children to drink socially is as useless as showing them how to eat candy in hopes of preventing diabetes.

Remember, too, the illegality of giving alcohol to a minor. In most states it is illegal for a minor to drink alcohol *anywhere*—even at home. Admittedly, chances are excellent that the authorities won't burst into your house on Thanksgiving or New Year's Day and cart you off because your child is sipping a glass of wine with dinner. But if you are encouraging—or overlooking—a minor's drinking at home, thereby breaking a law, you can't really be sure that he or she will respect this, or any other, law.

In spite of seeming evidence to the contrary, a parent *is* the most significant person in any child's life, an authority to whom a youngster looks for reference points and boundaries. Giving your child boundaries about drinking is like putting lines on a football field; it makes the game much easier to play intelligently. The attitudes in your household toward drinking—as well as other behaviors—strongly affect your child's decisions, both now and later in life.

Your child needs parents. And being a parent sometimes means setting guidelines your son or daughter may not agree with. So be it. Your taking care of your responsibilities as a parent is more important to your child's maturing process than your being a pal. We have seen numerous cases in which a parent, trying to be a best friend instead, turned a child on to alcohol. When the son or daughter began abusing alcohol, the parent asked, "Where did I go wrong?"

Rather than establishing a curriculum to teach a youngster to drink, parents might learn the symptoms of chemical dependency, including alcoholism, and where to go for help if the need should arise. Studying the problem and instituting valid treatment programs warrant more attention, at least until any prevention program proves successful.

Should parents drink in the presence of their children? This is a personal decision. In no way do I favor prohibition. To drink or not to drink is up to each individual *adult*.

If parents are honest with themselves, they may find that they allow children to drink because they, the parents, drink, and may feel inconsistent and hypocritical instructing the youngster not to use alcohol in the home. This is not a valid reason. Adults make house rules. Because a parent feels like drinking—and does—in no way assures a child the same right. For a minor and a dependent, living in *your* house, *you* lay down the boundaries. What parents do in their own house is their own business. Since when does a child have to approve of parental decisions?

At the heart of the issue is not *if* a parent drinks, but *how*. Parents who drink until they pass out, get sick all over the Christmas tree or otherwise imbibe irresponsibly set up implicit standards of consumption for their children. With this kind of adult model, drunkenness, not responsible drinking, becomes the "normal" and accepted standard.

Parents, if they drink, can demonstrate sensible drinking habits, which serve to establish acceptable guidelines within their family. Their example of social drinking—rather than out-of-control or excessive drinking—can be a reference point for a young person once he or she begins using alcohol. If he or she varies from those limits and begins abusing alcohol, parents' social-drinking models provide comparisons for his/her own drinking patterns.

But to assume that just because parents are social, reasonable drinkers their offspring will not have a problem with alcohol is erroneous and dangerous. This attitude can set up an automatic denial mechanism in both parent and child, blinding all parties to the realities of problem drinking.

Statistics show that teens and preteens coming from homes where parents drink socially have an above average chance of becoming problem drinkers. *That risk increases if one or both parents has a drinking problem.* (Over fifty percent of the young people in one particular residential treatment program for chemically dependent youth have one or both parents who are also chemically dependent.) There are, however, legions of alcoholics whose parents never had a problem with alcohol at all.

A significant example for a youngster is the parent who has had a problem with alcohol, who faced it and learned to live sober. This demonstrates a principle. A life-saving one: Once a person is hooked, the only answer is abstinence. To carry this further, once hooked on any kind of drug, the only answer is abstinence from *all* mood-changing drugs, including alcohol.

Nonalcoholic parents drink socially because that is what they are, social drinkers. Adults who have trouble drinking responsibly in front of their children had better examine their own drinking. Chances are that they have edged over into the problem-drinking zone without realizing it.

Until such time as a worthwhile alcohol prevention program comes into being, all parents can do is to drink responsibly themselves (if they drink), refrain from starting their minor children off on alcohol use at home, learn what they can about alcohol (and other drug) abuse and be on the alert for any symptoms of problem drinking in their children.

8

How Will I Know If My Child Has An Alcohol Problem?

"We are convinced to a man that alcoholics of our type are in the grip of a progressive illness. Over any considerable period we get worse, never better."

Alcoholics Anonymous, Second Edition.

☆ ☆ ☆

"There are more alcoholics in the San Francisco metropolitan area than heroin addicts in the entire United States."

Joel Fort, M.D.,
Alcohol: Our Biggest Drug Problem

☆ ☆ ☆

Rick, age seventeen, claimed that the only reason he was attending our group was that he had neglected to fix the tail light on his car and was cited. When questioned, he admitted that his .20 blood alcohol count (.10 qualifies a person for drunk driving in California) might have had something to do with his being there. It was his third arrest for drunk driving.

☆   ☆   ☆

What do parents, teachers, or any other adults who work with children, do when they suspect a preteen or teen may be having trouble with alcohol (or, for that matter, any other mood-changing drug)?

If you are a parent, you will doubtless have your private moments of hand-wringing, as you are struck by successive waves of fury, sadness, resentment, guilt, panic and feelings of inadequacy and helplessness.

If you are a teacher, you will have some of the same feelings of helplessness, especially if you are unsure of what that parent's reactions will be to the problem.

A major obstacle to detecting alcohol abuse among teens and preteens—besides the denial of the problem by the alcohol-respecting adult world—was that until a few years ago there was no screening device to help determine whether a young person's drinking was out of control. The self-testing measures used, the Johns Hopkins Twenty Questions and the National Council on Alcoholism test, were aimed exclusively at the adult population. A twelve- or thirteen-year-old could hardly be expected to relate to such questions as, "Do you occasionally drink when the boss gives you a hard time?" or "Have you tried to control your drinking by making a change in jobs, or moving to a new location?" or "Is drinking interfering with your marriage?"

It is not possible to measure the drinking of a child or adolescent by adult standards. So universal standards signifying alcohol abuse among this younger age group need to be established.

Since it is the symptoms or manifestations of problem drinking among youth that first attract attention, the questionnaires which help evaluate the problem are based on symptomatic indicators.

For any adults who live or work with adolescents and who need help in assessing whether a young person might be headed for, or already involved in, problem drinking, the tests given in this chapter may serve as measuring devices.

Two of these, the At Risk Youth Diagnostic Screening Device, especially for preteens, and the Youth Diagnostic Screening Device for Problem Drinkers, for high school ages, are an outgrowth of our Orange County survey on youth drinking patterns.* For the first time, in these two tests, factors are included which have actually been shown in a study of youth drinking to correlate with problem drinking.

Two other tests, a Twenty Questions for Youth, put together by the Alcoholism Council of Orange County, and a Twenty Questions for Parents who suspect a child may be in trouble with alcohol, are based on the experience of those working in the field of alcoholism diagnosis and treatment.

At Risk Youth Diagnostic Screening Device

As far as we are able to determine, this is the first test based on an actual study of youth drinking patterns which offers, for preteens, certain predictors for potential problem drinking. This device needs more study, application and follow-up. But from our survey of 2,500 youngsters in Orange County, several consequential and pathological clues to problem drinking surfaced—personality habit patterns and environmental detectors which relate to the development of problem drinking in an individual. Any youth who shows signs of these personality habits and early stage consequences can be considered at high risk for problem drinking later in adolescence or early adulthood.

The At Risk Youth Diagnostic Screening Device for pre-teens could be an important tool in intercepting potential problem drinkers, and thus lead to a prevention program *before* the youngster becomes deeply enmeshed in the web of alcoholism. In essence, we move the detection of alcoholism

---

*The At Risk Youth Diagnostic Screening Device for Problem Drinkers (preteens) and the Youth Diagnostic Screening Device for Problem Drinkers (teens) have been employed in the testing of over 10,000 youngsters in Minnesota, California, New York, Washington and Michigan.

or problem drinking upstream, hopefully getting to a young drinker *before* certain habit patterns of addiction have been so solidified that they require more intensive treatment or incarceration. This device could be instrumental in preventing early, middle or late stages of alcoholism.

As researchers Jessor and Jessor have demonstrated (see references, following the study in Part Two) if a preteen drinks, he or she is most likely at risk for problem drinking, has a greater chance (than a non-drinker) of developing a serious drinking problem by high school age.

This screening device is explained in more detail in Part Two, which includes the full report of the Orange County Study of Youth Drinking Patterns.

At Risk Youth Diagnostic Screening Device (for preteens)

(See also Part Two, pages 182 through 183.)

1. Are you male or female? (No score)
2. How old are you? (No score)
3. Have you ever lived with anyone other than your parents?
4. Do you usually have a job outside your home?
5. Do you go to church or another traditional religious institution? (Score 1 for "No")
6. Do you feel that you're on your own?
7. Does anyone in your family have a problem with drinking?
8. Did you have your first drink at home? (Score 1 for "No")
9. Do you sometimes turn off to people who give talks on alcoholism or drinking?
10. Do you believe drinking makes people more popular?
11. Have you ever gotten into trouble at school?
12. Do you get into trouble at school often?
13. Do you like school most of the time? (Score 1 for "No")

14. Do you generally get good grades in school? (Score 1 for "No")
15. Do you often have times when you're depressed or really down?
16. Would you say that you are a happy person? (Score 1 for "No")
17. Have you ever heard of Alateen?
18. Do you sometimes hang out with kids who drink? (Score 2 for "Yes")
19. Do you prefer to be with friends who drink? (Score 2 for "Yes")
20. Do you and your friends think sex and drinking go together? (Score 2 for "Yes")
21. Do you use or have you ever used drugs? (Score 2 for "Yes")
22. Do you favor pot over alcohol? (Score 2 for "Yes")
23. Do you smoke cigarettes regularly? (Score 2 for "Yes")
24. Have you ever been busted for possession of an illegal drug? (Score 2 for "Yes")
25. Have you ever gotten into trouble with the police? (Score 2 for "Yes")
26. Would you sometimes like to be a person who drinks? (Score 2 for "Yes")
27. Have you ever had a drink of beer, wine, or liquor *more than two or three times in your life?* (Score 2 for "Yes")

Unless otherwise indicated beside the question, all questions are to be given a score of 1 for a "Yes" response. The questions given a score of 2 for a "Yes" response were found to relate more significantly to problem drinking. (See page 181 of Part Two.) Scores on this test will range from 0 to 35. National studies suggest that those elementary and junior high school children who score in the upper percentiles (18 and above) are prime candidates for problem drinking education and prevention strategies. (See Part E, pages 188-193 for suggested programs of early intervention.)

Youth Diagnosis Screening Device for Problem Drinkers

For teen problem drinkers (high school age), we have developed a Youth Diagnostic Screening Device for Problem Drinkers (see also page 186 of Part Two). The purpose of this test is to determine those teens who have already reached problem levels in their drinking. Questions, again, are based on those items in our youth drinking survey which were found to correlate most highly with problem drinking.

Youth Diagnostic Screen Device for Problem Drinkers

1. Are you male or female? (No score.)
2. How old are you? (No score.)
3. Do you use or have you ever used drugs?
4. Have you ever been busted for possession of an illegal drug?
5. Have you had a drink of beer, wine, or liquor *more than two or three times in your life?*
6. Do you consider yourself as a person who drinks?
7. Do you favor pot over alcohol?
8. Do you and your friends think sex and drinking go together?
9. Do you sometimes hang out with kids who drink?
10. Do you prefer to be with friends who drink?
11. Do you sometimes drink because it makes you feel more at ease on a date?
12. Do you sometimes drink because it makes you feel more relaxed with the opposite sex?
13. Do you sometimes drink because it makes you feel better around people?
14. Do you sometimes drink because it helps you forget your worries?
15. Do you sometimes drink because it helps to cheer you up when you're in a bad mood?
16. Do you sometimes drink to change the way you feel?
17. Do you sometimes drink because it makes you feel stronger?

18. Have you ever borrowed money or done without other things to buy alcohol?
19. Have you ever skipped meals while drinking?
20. Do you sometimes gulp down a drink rather than drink it slowly?
21. Do you sometimes drink before going to a party?
22. Do you ever notice that your hands shake when you wake up in the morning?
23. Have you ever taken a drink in the morning?
24. Have you ever felt guilty or bummed out after drinking?
25. Do you ever have times when you cannot remember some of what happened while drinking (Score 2 for "Yes")
26. Have you ever stayed high drinking for a whole day? (Score 2 for "Yes")
27. Do you ever get mad or get into a heated argument when you drink?
28. Have you ever gotten into a fight when drinking?
29. Do you sometimes drink until there's nothing left to drink? (Score 2 for "Yes")
30. Would you say that you get "high" when you drink more than half the time? (Score 2 for "Yes")
31. Would you say that you get "drunk" or "bombed" at least once a month or more? (Score 2 for "Yes")
32. Have you had anything to drink in the last week?
33. When you drink, do you usually end up having more than four of whatever you're drinking? (Score 2 for "Yes")
34. Would you say that you have a drink of beer, wine, or liquor at least once a week or more? (Score 2 for "Yes")
35. Have you ever missed school or missed a class because of drinking? (Score 2 for "Yes")
36. Have you ever gotten into trouble at home because of your drinking?
37. Have you ever gotten into trouble outside your home because of your drinking?

38. Have you ever gotten into trouble with the police because of drinking?
39. Do you sometimes get drunk when you didn't start out to get drunk?
40. Do you sometimes try to cut down on your drinking?

Score all items 1 for "Yes" response unless otherwise indicated. Scores will range from 0 to 44. An *alcoholic* scores at least 3 on the nondrinking items (3-8), *and* at least 5 on the pathological style items (9-28 and 39-40), *and* at least 4 on the problematic consumption items (29-34), *and* at least 2 on the consequences items (35-38). (An *alcoholic* is problematic on all three problem drinking components [drinking style, consumption and consequences].) For a more detailed breakdown of scoring criteria and problem drinking components, see pages 183-186 of Part Two. A *problem drinker* (but *not* an alcoholic) scores at least 3 on the nondrinking items, and scores the same as that required for an alcoholic diagnosis on *two of the three* problem drinking components. A *potential problem drinker* scores at least 3 on the nondrinking items, and scores the same as that required for an alcoholic diagnosis on *one* of the three problem drinking components.

Twenty Questions For Parents

The following questions have been devised for parents who suspect a child or adolescent is having trouble with alcohol. Symptoms may vary with each young person, but there are certain universal tipoffs. Here are a few:

1. Does your child's drinking behavior match any of the warning signals referred to in the teen or preteen screening devices?
2. Is your liquor supply dwindling? If your child is abusing alcohol, your stock might evaporate mysteriously or turn into colored water. Unless you keep an inventory of your liquor, such practices could go on undetected for months.
3. Has your child's personality changed noticeably? Does he or she exhibit sudden mood swings, such as out-of-the-ordinary irritability, giddiness, depression, unprovoked hostility?

4. Is he or she becoming less responsible? About doing chores, for example, getting home on time, following instructions and household rules?

5. Has interest waned in school work, school or extra-curricular activities, athletics? Are grades dropping? A frequent hint is a lowering of the level of performance in school. The child may become truant or drop out altogether. Negativity sets in; nothing goes right.

6. Does your child seem to be losing old friends and hanging out with a drinking and/or partying group? All social life for the young problem drinker begins to center around drinking, occasions for drinking and alcohol-abusing friends. He or she has no time for non-abusing friends, but trades down on former friends and seeks out those with similar drinking habits. A young alcoholic must do this, to justify his or her own alcohol abuse.

   Often parents find out about their youngster's drinking from long-time friends or schoolmates—those who no longer seem to be friends.

7. Are you missing money or objects that could be converted to cash? A young alcoholic has an increasingly expensive addiction to maintain. Eventually the need for alcohol overcomes any guilt about stealing from family members, friends or anyone else.

8. Do you hear consistently from neighbors, friends or others about your child's drinking or questionable behaviors? An alcoholic youngster's reputation suffers. Listen to these reports. There may be substance to them.

9. Is your child in trouble with the law? Even one arrest for an alcohol-related offense is a red flag that may well signal alcoholism. Kids that don't have drinking problems don't get arrested for crimes or other offenses committed while drinking.

   If a young person is arrested for an alcohol-related offense or was drinking at the time when he or she committed a crime, you can bet the rent there were similar other occasions when he or she was not caught.

10. Does your child or adolescent vehemently defend his or her right to drink, react belligerently to comments or criticisms about his or her drinking habits? If so, there is a good chance the young person is abusing alcohol. People defend strongly that which has become very important to them.

11. Does your child turn off to talks about alcohol or alcoholism? Adolescent alcohol abusers "stick the bananas in their ears" rather than hear anything that might interfere with their drinking habits. The non-abusing kid doesn't care one way or the other.

12. Does your child get into fights with other youngsters? Problem-drinking youths are apt to have altercations with others—both young people and adults. Over seventy percent of all beatings, stabbings and assaults take place when one or both participants have been drinking.

13. Are there signs of medical or emotional problems? Be on the lookout for ulcers, high blood pressure, acute indigestion, gastritis, depression, liver dysfunction, kidney problems—and, of course, injuries from alcohol-related accidents.

14. Does he or she drive irresponsibly? Those in trouble with alcohol are known hazards on the highway. They may also lie about where they are taking the car, make excuses for not getting it home on time and even hot-wire it late at night for joyrides with friends.

15. Is your child generally dishonest? Not telling the truth goes hand in hand with problem drinking. For young alcoholics, lying becomes so automatic that they come up with fibs even when they don't need them, when the truth would have served them just as well. There is a saying, "Young alcoholics have two things in common. They have a terminal attack of the cool and are stuck in sneak gear."

16. Does your child volunteer to clean up after adult cocktail parties, but neglect other chores? This sounds like a small point, but it is surprising how many young drinkers use this ploy, and how slow parents are to catch on. Draining half-empty glasses after an adult gathering is a cheap high.

17. Do you find obvious signs, like a stash of bottles in the bedroom or garage? Parents of a young alcoholic are always astounded at what they find during a thorough housecleaning. Kids that don't have a problem with alcohol don't make a practice of hiding bottles under their mattresses, in the speakers of their stereos, behind insulation in garages or in the water tanks of toilets. Even the ones who are the foggiest from drinking manage to be ingenious about hiding places.

18. Do you detect physical signs—alcohol on the breath, for instance? One adolescent told us he had come home almost every night for six months reeking so strongly that his parents could have chinned themselves on his breath. They had been too busy to notice. They finally got the message when a school counselor advised them that their son had been suspended from school for being drunk in class. Polydrug users (those who mix drugs, usually including alcohol) exhibit other telltale signs, too —like a change in the size of pupils in the eyes, hyperactivity or sluggishness, slurred or incoherent speech. These are all clues which should not be ignored.

19. Does your child spend a lot of time alone closed in a bedroom or recreation room, bursting forth now and then only to disappear out the door? ("Where are you going?" "Out.") Does he or she seem to resent your questions about destinations and activities? A certain amount of this mystery, aloofness and resentment is, of course, typical of adolescence. When it is carried to an extreme, you should be aware that it could mean problems with alcohol or other drugs.

20. Has your child's relationships with other family members deteriorated? A young person's ability to relate to others effectively is impaired by alcohol, and the first relationships to suffer are those within the family. A young alcoholic will try to avoid family gatherings— occasions he or she once enjoyed—particularly if faced with doting or critical relatives whose expectations often make the young person feel guilty and uncomfortable.

In short, an alcohol abusing youngster's life changes, begins to revolve around drinking. More and more of the individual's energy and ingenuity goes into procuring and drinking alcohol. The out-of-control drinker becomes a stranger, a source of frustration, irritation and disruption to other family members. Alcohol abuse can create Mr. Hydes out of seemingly happy kids and isolate them from those who love them.

Twenty Questions for Youth

The following Twenty Questions for Youth has proved to be a questionnaire that a young person can understand and relate to, a measuring device he or she can take unsupervised and answer anonymously. The questions imply a certain set of drinking standards. Any deviations from this standard signify that a youth might be heading for trouble with alcohol. Many schools in southern California and other parts of the nation have made these available on handout sheets to their students.

1. Do you lose time from school due to drinking?
2. Do you drink to feel more comfortable?
3. Do you drink to build self-confidence?
*4. Do you drink alone?
*5. Is drinking affecting your reputation?
*6. Do you drink to escape from study or home worries?
7. Do you feel guilty or bummed out after drinking?

*8. Does it bother you if someone says you drink too much?

9. Do you feel more at ease on a date when drinking?

10. Have you gotten into trouble at home because of your drinking?

11. Do you borrow money or "do without" other things to buy alcohol?

12. Do you feel a sense of power when you drink?

*13. Have you lost friends since you started drinking?

*14. Do your friends drink less than you do?

15. Have you started hanging out with a heavy-drinking crowd?

16. Do you drink until the wine, beer or hard liquor is all gone?

17. Do you ever wake up and wonder what happened the night before?

18. Have you ever been busted or hospitalized due to drinking?

*19. Do you turn off to any studies or lectures about alcohol abuse?

*20. Do you think you have a problem with alcohol?

---

*Further testing and clinical study have shown that these questions have less significance in determining a drinking problem among youth (Author's note, 1979).

The teen or preteen is asked to figure his or her own score on this test. The instructions are as follows: Each question you have answered with "Yes" is a warning signal of problem drinking. Even one "Yes" indicates you could have a problem with alcohol. If three or more questions describe your drinking, you could be headed for serious trouble with alcohol. But it can be avoided, as alcoholism can be intercepted and treated. This quiz is based on a similar test prepared by Johns Hopkins University Hospital to determine alcoholism.

This questionnaire is by no means an absolute method of diagnosing problem drinking or alcoholism. None of the tests given here indicate *for certain* whether a young person is — or is going to be — in trouble with alcohol. But they are clue-givers. Of the four, the At Risk Diagnostic Screening Device (preteens) and the Youth Diagnostic Screening Device (teens) are the most scientific—based on an actual study.

The Twenty Questions for Youth is, however, an opportunity for young people to give some thought to their alcohol consumption and its consequences. It also sets a standard for social drinking. When we hand these out, we include a phone number, too, which they can call for further information or help. At the Orange County Council on Alcoholism offices, we have had numerous calls from teens, preteens and parents, who, after looking over this test, decided to find out more about alcoholism. School nurses and counselors hand it out to students they suspect might be abusing alcohol. Several members of our youth group joined the program as a direct result of taking this test in school.

A parent can make the youth tests available, but it is important that your child answer his or her test questions privately. Unless the results are volunteered, it is best for parents not to ask. Badgering by parents, teachers, friends or members of the clergy has little positive effect, and may have a negative one. When plagued by a parent or any other authority figure, a young problem drinker is likely to deny the problem by strongly understating his or her drinking. Then a great deal of energy and time go into fortifying that denial, and the young person ignores the real issue—his or her drinking pattern.

The young individual who comes to the realization independently that drinking is at the core of his or her problems is more apt to seek help than one who is nagged or driven into it.

9

Tough Love and
Other Tips for Parents

"As long as you've got your parents screaming at you, have at it. But once they stop yelling, brace yourself. You've lost your favorite toys and they're ready to deal with your behavior. They're through talking about it." Kip Heinold, Associate Director of the Family Development Program, Inc., Laguna Beach, California, working with a group of problem youngsters.

☆   ☆   ☆

"Science has proven insanity is hereditary. Parents get it from their kids." Sign at Juvenile Hall in Orange, California.

☆   ☆   ☆

Most parents simply do not know how to handle an alcoholic offspring. None of the parenting manuals or psychology texts have prepared them for coping with an addicted youth. The kid defies all logic and reason. Each time things seem to be getting better, the young alcoholic tears up the landscape again.

I have known parents, in a panicky attempt at straightening out a young abuser, to lock the kid in a room, only to find an empty room with an open window the next morning.

One mother, trying to prevent her preteenage son from helping himself to her money, wrapped her wallet in a Baggie and took it into the shower with her each morning.

Parents are afraid to invite their own friends into their home, for fear of an ugly scene with their alcohol-abusing child. They cease going on vacations; the alcoholic is too unbearable to take along, and they are afraid if they leave him or her home alone the house will be demolished from one continuous party.

Then there is the disappointment and degradation father feels when he has to bail his son out of a juvenile detention center, the awful anxiety mother feels when a voice on the phone advises her that her daughter has been in an accident, arrested for drunk driving or found wandering along a street, drunk and half-clothed.

Clearly when youngsters become alcoholic (or dependent on other chemicals) they are not living in their parents' homes; the parents are living in the children's.

Once you have established the fact that, yes, your child does have a problem with alcohol, what do you do? Let's start with some don'ts.

DON'T confront your youngster about drinking *while* he or she is under the influence. Nothing is gained. It's like talking to a wall and could lead to an ugly scene.

DON'T make excuses to your spouse, family, friends or school authorities for your youngster's drinking. This includes writing notes to cover up tardiness or unexcused absences from school. Alcohol abuse needs to be faced squarely. Wishing it away—or waiting for it to vanish—doesn't work. Covering for the alcoholic only prolongs his or her dilemma.

DON'T take responsibility for your child's drinking problem. The young alcoholic is sick and needs counseling and treatment. Alcoholism is a disease, like tuberculosis or diabetes, and parental guilt has never proved to be a remedy. If anything, it tends to hinder an alcoholic's recovery. A parent's job is to get the alcohol-abusing child into treatment. Whether or not the child responds to treatment is out of the parent's control.

DON'T accept as normal behavior a drunken son or daughter who comes home and destroys the house or creates havoc within the family. Try to respond objectively, as if this wild creature were a stranger. (This is obviously a tough assignment.) What parents fail to see, because of their emotional involvement, is that if their children were to treat anyone else in the community like they treat their own mothers and fathers, they would probably be locked up. If the youngster exhibits violence—or even threatens it—call the authorities to remove the offender from the premises.

DON'T nag or scream at an adolescent about drinking. It certainly won't make the drinker quit or cut down. Your anger might even provide an added excuse to get drunk. Besides, the young alcoholic doesn't have to worry about his or her drinking problem; *you* are doing it instead!

DON'T clean up your alcohol-abusing child's messes and predicaments. It is important for the abuser to see just what alcohol is doing to him or her, to realize it is the number one problem.

The more unpleasant and painful the consequences of drinking behavior are, the more desirable it becomes to stop drinking. No one surrenders a behavior when it seems to be working—even if the activity is destructive drinking. In the language of chemical dependency, this is known as raising the alcoholic's bottom (the bottom that must be reached before he or she realizes that there is no way to go but up, and therefore starts to face the drinking problem). This may be allowing the young alcoholic the *privilege* (and it is!) of paying the fines, losing the driver's license, or, if need be, spending some time in a juvenile hall or detention center. The sooner the youth links the trouble with drinking, the greater his or her chance of dealing with it. Overprotective parents unwittingly can steer a young alcoholic into an early grave.

An essential point to remember is that when parents take responsibility for their son's or daughter's drinking behavior, or assume guilt because he or she is drinking, they almost invariably jump in and clean up the wreckage. Then the young person doesn't have to. Some alcoholism programs call this "enabling." You are enabling the alcoholic to continue the drinking and the drinking behavior.

The term "tough love" means letting your children get themselves out of the jams they got themselves into. Parents, acting out of misplaced responsibility and guilt, often keep their youngsters from facing their drinking and doing something about it. We knew one father who had spent nearly $15,000 on his son's fines, lawyers' fees, restitutions, thefts, hot checks and repairs on crashed autos. As the father kept jumping in and bailing him out, the son's drinking worsened. And the father almost bankrupted the family.

Far better that the alcohol-abusing young person learn at age fourteen or fifteen how the crime-and-punishment sequence works, rather than waiting another ten years — even if it means spending time in a juvenile center or a youth forestry camp making picnic tables. If a parent denies an alcohol-abusing child the privilege of paying his or her dues, the problem invariably gets worse. Compared with a penitentiary, a juvenile center is a country club. And prisons have turned into permanent homes for many alcoholics.

If the young alcoholic decides to steal alcohol or the money to buy it, don't be afraid to let the gears of justice grind over the offender. Be assured that if your adolescent is blowing it in the community — getting into illegal activities — he or she had better be prepared for the consequences. It's called spitting into the wind.

DON'T let yourself be so ruled by the kid's alcoholic behavior that you let it pull your own behavior down, too. Avoid screaming arguments. By doing this, you are preserving your alcohol-abusing child's right to bear his or her own burdens. When parents fight and argue with their alcoholic youngster, they are reflecting the child's behavior and assuming his or her lousy feelings. This lets the young abuser off the hook. If your alcoholic juvenile is allowed to keep his or her own uncomfortable, bad feelings, he or she eventually will get sick of them and seek alternate ways of living. Among those alternatives is sobriety.

By staying clear of the young alcoholic's pit of despair and discomfort and bad behavior, parents offer a reference point, a plateau to rise to. By establishing a firm attitude and refusing to collect the kid's "garbage," parents give the young drinker nothing to resist, so he or she is left to face the issue honestly.

DON'T view your child as lacking backbone or will power. An alcoholic is in the throes of a disease, one that kills. You can be sure it takes truckloads of will and strength to lie and scheme and steal, just to hold things together so he or she can continue to drink. Abusing alcohol requires a lot of negative energy, but energy nonetheless. We often ask parents of an alcoholic youngster, "If you think will power works on a disease, try it sometime on diarrhea."

DON'T assume your child doesn't love you because of the way he or she acts when drinking. The alcoholic youth has no choice. It is not a question of being unloving; the young alcoholic is simply unable to love anyone, for the time being. Those who don't like themselves are not capable of loving others. What young people have to offer parents and others is very much based on what they think of themselves—and alcoholics, in spite of their frequent boasts and grandiose claims, tend to have low opinions of themselves.

DON'T be angry with your alcoholic child, if you can help it. If you need to show your anger, direct it at what the child does, not at the child. Try to see the young person as separate from his or her actions. By venting your frustration on the young alcoholic, you reinforce his or her negative self-image or, as mentioned earlier, absolve the youth from assuming responsibility for his or her drinking behavior. Remember, by this time the kid is drinking out of control and can't help what he or she is doing. Young alcoholics seldom understand the nature of their problems.

DON'T be patronizing or indulgent. It doesn't work. Simply expect your youngster to live by the rules of your house and hope he or she can get on top of the problem. This way, you are helping your alcohol-abusing child become uncomfortable with his or her drinking, *in a firm, but loving way*, without either malice or frothy sympathy. We tell the young members of our group, "If you're looking for sympathy, you'll find it in the dictionary, between shit and syphilis. Not here.

"But if you want to find out how to quit drinking and get yourself a better deal out of life, then you're in the right place."

Much of the adults' lives are absorbed with trying to handle one drinking-related catastrophe after another. Caught in a paralysis of not knowing what to do, parents spend their time holding their breaths and waiting to react to the next crisis. They have given over control of their lives to their addicted child. They have allowed themselves to be tyrannized in their own homes.

If a youngster is arrested for being drunk, most parents panic and rush to the rescue, blaming themselves for what they did or did not do in the child-raising process. But guilt never solved anything. In reality, no one is to blame because someone begins drinking alcoholically. A parent's effectiveness in bringing up a child has not been proved to be a determinant of whether that child becomes a problem drinker instead of a social drinker. Young people get drunk because they drink alcohol.

Finding out why a problem drinker abuses alcohol is not the solution—and probing into the intricacies of personal why's and wherefore's has minimal value in helping an alcoholic. (In fact, it may even give him or her an excuse to keep on drinking.)

What is most important is how parents handle the realization that they have an alcohol-abuser living in their house, not what went on in the past.

Parents often become so locked into their children's addictions that they are cast in the roles of perpetual saviors, continually spending money and energy bailing them out.

Reliving their parenthood—trying to figure out how they could have done something differently when the child was five years old—can turn parents into basket cases. Pushed to the extreme, it could be the youngster's turn to watch Mom do the "Thorazine shuffle" in some mental institution or monitor Dad and his life-sustaining equipment in the coronary care unit of a hospital.

"Tough love" means setting the rules for the child's behavior in the house (this is also called protecting your environment) and letting the young person work out his or her own problems at school or with the law. We ask parents to affirm to themselves that their alcoholic children's actions in the community will be dealt with appropriately. In other words, divorce yourself from your alcoholic child.

One mother we knew took her son to class and sat next to him to be sure he made it to school. But as soon as mother left, so did junior—off to the playground to get drunk.

Let your child find out how the school system deals with kids who would rather party than go to school, or who can't make it to classes because they're sick from partying the night before. The system may work slowly—but it works.

DON'T play amateur detective; following your offspring around the town to see what he or she is into is a waste of your time and your strength. Hiding in the bushes, tailing your son or daughter at night with your car lights off, steaming open the mail—all those sneaky manifestations of the parent-sleuth syndrome—only serve to snag the parent into the young alcoholic's emotional traps. You simply produce arguments over where he or she was supposed to be, who was there, etc. Cross-examination and triumphs of discovery (aHA, I caught you!) do nothing but set up games between you and your child and take the young drinker's attention away from the fact that he or she is going down the tubes! All this gives the kid another excuse to blame the problems on parents, rather than looking at his or her drinking.

DON'T give an alcohol-abusing youngster any money, except for a minimal allowance. It would doubtless go for wine, liquor or beer. Let the young person figure out how to get drinking money, or know what it's like to go hungry after spending lunch money on alcohol.

DON'T make threats you're not prepared to back up. When parents promise their young drinker that they will call the authorites the next time he or she comes home drunk or abusive and then backs down when it happens, they disappoint the young person and prevent him or her from experiencing the crime-punishment sequence. In essence, they rob him or her of the chance to "bottom out." As parents, you also stand to lose a valuable asset—your credibility. Why should your youngster ever believe you, if you don't carry through with your threats?

A parent ought to take action, not simply issue warnings or talk about what is *going* to happen sometime in the dim future if the kid doesn't straighten out. The youth has been threatened plenty of times, knows the words of your parental lectures by heart. Our advice to parents: "Demonstrate, don't ventilate."

What can a parent of a young alcohol abuser do to improve the situation?

Here are some specific steps parents can take to isolate the young alcoholic's drinking and diffuse a volatile atmosphere in the home.

First, find out all you can about the disease of alcoholism. Attend some Al-Anon meetings (an adjunct of AA for family members or those who live with alcoholics). Here you can learn to better understand your alcoholic child and your own reactions. You will discover that there are plenty of others who have survived the anxieties and heartaches of alcoholic progeny. Sharing experiences and feelings with others like you will strengthen your resolve and help keep you sane. Unless those close to alcoholics (some call these people co-alcoholics or mirror alcoholics) get help themselves, they can get just as sick as the alcohol abusers. Alcoholism becomes a family disease.

If you strongly suspect your child has a drinking problem, get him or her to a doctor—not just any available doctor, or even your trusted family physician—*but a doctor who understands alcoholism*. If you are not sure of your doctor's knowledge of the disease, call a local Alcoholics Anonymous central office or regional chapter of the National Council on Alcoholism. They have lists of doctors who understand chemical dependency and the symptoms of alcohol abuse and won't prescribe other drugs to cover them up, which could lead to your child's trading one addiction for another. The number of prescriptions written to alcoholics for tranquilizers and barbiturates attest to the fact that many doctors really don't understand the problem. But those doctors with experience in treating alcoholics are quick to recognize the symptoms and have helped plenty of young alcoholics see their drinking for what it is.

Adolescents show a dualism in attitudes toward their bodies. On one hand, they scream about pollution, insist on eating food with no preservatives and revolt against contamination of our waterways—all good and noble thoughts. On the other hand, many of them treat their bodies like garbage pails by pouring truckloads of alcohol and other drugs down their throats. Sometimes a doctor's frankness about what a young alcohol abuser is doing to his body plays into the kid's vanity—and just might work to save his or her life.

Learn what treatment facilities—residential or outpatient —are available near you for the young alcoholic. Visit these facilities or programs and find out how they work, whether there are waiting lists, how treatment can be financed, especially if it is residential. Some of these facilities or programs may help you with an evaluation of the seriousness of your child's alcohol problem.

The best form of therapy for alcoholics, young or old, male or female, is Alcoholics Anonymous (AA)—and programs which are based on the AA Steps and tenets. Nearly one million alcoholics are members of AA. Your local AA central office or intergroup can tell you if there is a young people's meeting near you, or a meeting of mixed ages which includes several young people.

The AA office also can arrange for a young, sober alcoholic to come by your house and talk with your youngster or take him/her to an AA meeting. If the child resists this personal approach, give him or her the location and time of the AA meeting with instructions to attend.

If there is no young people's AA group in your area, call the local chapter of the National Council on Alcoholism. Many have groups for teen and preteen alcohol abusers. Or your county Mental Health office may know of resources for young alcoholics in your community.

The most successful programs seem to be those run by young, recovered chemically dependent people, who have the disease and have stopped drinking or using other drugs. Counselors who are chemically dependent and have found the way to their own comfortable sobriety seem to have an extra measure of rapport with young abusers of alcohol and other drugs.

You have the power to make it a condition of your child's living at home that he or she attend an alcohol awareness class or AA group. He or she may not accept the information about the disease immediately, but at least you have laid some important groundwork.

Choose an appropriate moment to suggest to your son or daughter that he or she seek help about drinking, namely *after* he or she has blown it in some way because of abusing alcohol. This misstep could involve coming home drunk, trouble at school because of drinking, drunk driving, or whatever. This way, the parents can key their instructions to a situation, a specific consequence that can be used as a direct reason for the young alcohol abuser to attend counseling or go into treatment. (Do wait, however, until the youngster sobers up to confront him or her. It's useless to try to reason with a drunken kid.)

Above all, try to detach yourself from your child's problem. Al-Anon has an excellent saying, "Let go and let God." Learning to release the young alcoholic frees the parents from the emotional blender they find themselves in. And it allows them to get on with the daily business of living with as little interference and disruption from their alcoholic youngster as possible.

Of course, there will be sadnesses and aggravations. A parent is not made of granite. But your child's gross drinking behavior doesn't have to wind you up like a cheap toy. *You don't have to make your youngster the source of your happiness or unhappiness.* You can learn to step aside when the alcoholic adolescent throws his emotional bucketful at the wall; don't stand there and let it hit you, or wallow in it or hurl it back at the kid. The parent, as the most significant person in any child's life, teaches—by example—the youngster how to deal with life. And if your lesson is titled, "How to Give People, Places and Things Ultimate Power Over Your Emotions," that is just what the child learns.

Don't overreact with relief and joy, or inflate the moment out of all proportion when your young drinker finally announces that he or she has decided to get help for a drinking problem. The youngster is merely trying to save his or her own hide. Drinking has become too painful and requires too much busyness, running back and forth to court, lawyers' offices and probation department appointments. The young alcoholic is kept in a harried state paying fines; sitting in a school counselor's office; getting thrown out of school; getting back into school; sneaking into the house at 4 a.m.; hiding from the police; getting caught by the police; getting up in the middle of the night to urinate; not getting up in the middle of the night to urinate—and all the other questionable joys that go along with drinking alcoholically.

Too much parental effusion robs the young people of the good feelings that come with doing something about their drinking—just as getting furious at them when they blow it takes away their rotten feelings. You wouldn't buy someone a new car because that person saved himself or herself from drowning or gave up burglarizing gas stations. These life-preserving decisions are not accompanied by bands and banners. The same principle of necessity is at work when a young alcoholic decides to quit drinking and straighten things out. Such decisions are made because they *have* to be made.

Show your love and your caring, while letting your youngster own the good feelings that accompany dealing with the drinking problem. And please don't come up with the "It's about time!" line. That makes as much sense as telling a cancer patient, "Well, it sure took you long enough to get over that cancer."

If your youngster happens to start drinking again, and you consequently withhold your love, you are placing conditions on your feelings, and again, you are giving your child control over your life. If your happiness is dependent on your alcoholic son's or daughter's behavior—drinking or otherwise—you are in for a ton of grief.

The young person's sobriety must be his or her own responsibility. Any youth, alcohol abusing or not, eventually must realize that the good decisions he or she makes in life result directly in his or her own well-being. They are not made to please parents, or anyone else. A comfortable home is a by-product, not a condition, of sobriety.

What a parent of a young alcoholic should aim to become is a wise referral agency—compassionate but nonmartyred—a mature person who can make suggestions about where to go for help.

10

For The Young Person Who Stops Drinking

"When you quit drinking, you find out who your friends are." Cindy, thirteen, sober member of Alcoholics Anonymous.

☆   ☆   ☆

Denny, fifteen, came to our group as a probation department referral. He had been arrested for driving under the influence of alcohol, although he was too young to have a driver's license.

His parents were confused about what to do with their youngest son. Their other children, a girl, seventeen, and a boy, sixteen, had caused them no loss of sleep.

Denny was a different story. He had been in and out of trouble since age eleven—the year he had started drinking. No matter how much they punished or even beat him, Denny continued to be beyond their control. They had considered placing him in a respite (foster) home; he was just too much for them to handle.

Denny and his parents attended our youth and parent groups respectively. Though he kept on drinking and getting into trouble for three more months, our real work during that time was done with his parents. They were able, finally, to back off from Denny's poor behavior around the house and began allowing him to clean up his own messes in the community. They felt better. Their own attitudes toward life were not so dependent on Denny's good or bad behavior. They rarely let Denny upset them with the burdens of *his* poor decisions. When they left Denny's problems to Denny, eventually he grew sick and tired of coping with the consequences of his drinking. In effect, they defogged the situation and isolated the drinking as the major problem.

Denny and his parents moved away, but they still write to us. Denny is doing well in school, and his attitude around home has improved. This is explained, in part, by the fact that he had received new information about alcohol and his own role in what had happened to him. A significant factor in Denny's improvement is that the move to a new location took him away from some strong negative peer influence.

In his last letter he said, "I haven't had anything to drink in three months. It just seemed to get in the way of my taking care of business. I wish I could tell my friends how it feels to make A's and B's in school and get along with my folks."

☆　☆　☆

Alcoholism has been called the lonely disease. The alcoholic carries his or her inner burdens alone, as alcohol begins to wall off loved ones, jobs, sports, hobbies, anything or anyone that stands in the way of drinking. Drinking may seem to be the membership card to a jolly fellowship—but alcoholism is not a team sport. The male or female whose drinking has reached the disease level is forced eventually into a solo operation. Wives, lovers, husbands, children, other family members, employers and friends usually are happy to put as much distance as possible between themselves and the practicing alcoholic.

For youngsters, alcoholism is less isolating. After all, parents are responsible for minor dependents until they reach eighteen years of age, so alcohol-abusing kids ordinarily don't lose their families—not unless their behavior becomes so uncontrolled and unacceptable that they are placed in foster homes or closed-care facilities.

As the Orange County and other recent surveys indicate, between seventy and ninety percent of teens and preteens drink alcohol, and over a third of those have reached at least beginning stage alcoholism. With fifteen to eighteen percent claiming to drink alone (occasionally), it appears that the majority of kids drink in flocks. They party together in an atmosphere that not only condones drunkenness but encourages it. Getting drunk is much more often tolerated among youths than adults. Anyone who has been on the fringes of a teen party or attended a rock concert knows that it seems to be the minority at such events who DON'T get drunk or loaded.

Youth doesn't require the ritual or the pretense for getting together to drink. Young people gather for the specific, announced purpose of drinking as much as they can. Of the 2,500 questioned in the Orange County study, thirty percent of those who drink said that when they drink they have more than three of whatever they are drinking. A full twenty-four percent admitted to drinking until the supply ran out.

Adults, on the other hand, attach non alcohol-related reasons and proper niceties to their drinking occasions. They call them business luncheons, dinner parties, cocktail suppers, fellowship gatherings, awards banquets, conventions, fund-raisers and benefits. And drunkenness, though usually overlooked or excused, is not encouraged. When an adult starts careening down the road of habitual drunkenness, friends and colleagues get on his/her case; the alcoholic behavior becomes unacceptable except to those who are heavy drinkers themselves.

For a young person, there is very little dissuading pressure from peers about drunkenness. Most of those friends are doing the same thing!

Abstinence, like alcoholism, can be lonely for anyone. But for a young recovering person—who may have started using the chemical in the first place to be one of the crowd—loneliness is magnified until it is almost unbearable. There is a camaraderie among problem drinking youth. The kid who has never used alcohol—or who has and quit—is hard pressed to find others the same age who don't drink. The abstainer is alienated from former friends, is sometimes ostracized for having "sold out" to adult authority. He or she is expected to party, encouraged to get drunk. Sobriety for a youngster can prove so lonely and painful that many abstainers or former abusers of alcohol ultimately find it easier to say yes to an offer to drink than to remain outside the circle of old friends.

The young recovering alcoholic or other drug addict is lucky indeed if he or she is in a school with a chemical dependency program, or a neighborhood with a youth half-way house, which can provide a core of sober kids and a necessary support group.

In our group at the Orange County Alcoholism Council, we work hard to help the newly sober youth fortify the resolve to abstain. Volunteer counselors include him or her in their activities, offer invitations to young people's AA meetings or dances for recovering young people. For the newly sober young person, it is a revelation to attend a party where two or three hundred abstaining contemporaries are having fun, on a natural high. These former drinkers have to learn to have fun without alcohol, and for many this takes time and ingenuity on their part and on the part of those who care about them.

The need to develop "alternate highs" has resulted in several youth alcoholism programs around the country incorporating rugged, outdoor activities in their schedules, like mountaineering and rock-climbing, which help the recovering youth find a valuable new sense of "self."

A great deal of time in our group is spent with the youngster who has quit drinking discussing the question, "What is a friend?" If honest, the young ex-drinker soon realizes that these so-called "friends" aren't really friends at all. The definition of "friend" gets a thorough going over. "Is it someone who encourages you to drink, when he or she knows alcohol is causing you serious problems?" "Or is it someone who looks out for your best interests, is sensitive to your needs, doesn't want to see you get into trouble?" Many newly sober young alcoholics can then begin to reassess their relationships. Most don't find it easy to maintain old friendships while sober. A few find their old partners boring; to be straight and sober in a room full of loaded and drunk kids is like standing in the produce department of a supermarket talking to turnips and melons.

Sadly, many kids don't see it that way. The deck is stacked against fourteen-year-old alcoholics who are trying to stay sober, find out who and what they are and still function in a society where ninety percent of their friends drink alcohol— especially when those friends attempt to convince them they can handle alcohol, even ridicule them for not drinking. It requires precious time for youngsters to realize that those who force drinks on them and make fun of their abstinence probably have drinking problems themselves.

We have had many young recovering alcoholics report back that their old friends no longer trusted them. Alcohol-abusing kids are generally into illegal activities of one sort or another, and they develop an instinctive paranoia, a natural distrust of anyone who doesn't do as they do.

We attempt to show the sober teen the virtues of exchanging the old drinking friends for new ones who are not abusing alcohol. These suggestions may help the young person who wants to remain abstinent but is having trouble dealing with peers who drink:

You don't have to make excuses when refusing a drink

If someone offers you a drink you don't want, keep your refusal simple. "No, thank you" suffices. It is not necessary to feel apologetic or to launch into a long discussion about why you don't drink. (The other person probably isn't that interested anyway.) The choice to drink or not is your business, and the briefer your explanation, the less attention you'll draw to your abstinence. If you are sober and intend to stay that way, you need to depend a lot on just one word— "no."

Don't tempt yourself

If you are newly sober and are uncomfortable at places where others are drinking, stay away from them. You don't have to put yourself through the experience. Better to pass up a few parties than to threaten your sobriety. When you are able to handle them more comfortably—and if you still want to participate—there will always be more parties. After you have attended a few while sober, you might change your mind about their appeal and opt for a different sort of entertainment.

Seek out new things to do

You will probably discover and enjoy some new activities and hobbies that don't revolve around drinking—or rediscover a few old ones you put away when they cut into your drinking time.

In most cities, young people's Alcoholics Anonymous groups sponsor dances and parties. You might try one:

they're fun—good bands, other kids your age enjoying each others' company without alcohol or other drugs. A call to the Alcoholics Anonymous central or intergroup office in your area will put you in touch with a young people's AA group.

Or you may find a discotheque near you that doesn't allow drinking. A few such places have opened specifically for sober teens who want to dance to good music without having to hassle with others who are drunk and obnoxious. And many churches sponsor get-togethers. You might be surprised at how much fun they can be.

The important thing to remember is that if you are a teen or preteen who doesn't drink or use other drugs, you are not alone. There are others like you, having a good time without mind-benders. And there are alternatives to booze parties. Check around.

When a young alcoholic gets sober and goes about taking care of business, the quality of life improves. Healthy relationships are developed with family and friends. You begin to take better care of your physical self, get back into sports and other activities. The young recovering person really has something to offer others. A happy, creative and productive life is a far greater attraction for abstinence than all the sermonizing you can deliver. The message comes through: Because you stop drinking, it's not the end of your life. Just the opposite, in fact—it's the beginning.

Don't put down the ones who drink

You will hear it said that there is nothing more self-righteous than a reformed drunk. It's the finger-shaking brand of abstinence by a former problem drinker that turns people off. With missionary zeal, this reformer tries to get everyone else to climb on the same abstinence wagon and ends up being a friendless boor. Whether to drink or not is a personal choice. And getting along in this drinking society of ours requires patience and more than a little tolerance.

Friends with drinking problems of their own will probably be curious about the positive changes in your life. They will want to know more about how you manage to live sober — and enjoy it. Often friends will ask the sober alcoholic — the one who isn't into fire and brimstone and white-knuckled, tight-lipped sobriety — for help with their drinking problems. It happens all the time.

Think twice about climbing into a drinking friend's car

This advice goes for anyone. Even small amounts of alcohol impair a person's ability to drive an automobile. This impairment is often more pronounced with young drivers, since they generally weigh less than adults and feel the effects of alcohol faster.

Tests among professional race drivers showed that after a few drinks they had difficulty handling their automobiles, *even though they believed they were in complete control.*

Drinking drivers account for more than half of all highway fatalities. You are taking a chance by riding with a friend who has been drinking, since judgment, reaction time, reflexes and eyesight unquestionably have been affected by alcohol — even though it may not seem that way. *Don't be afraid to refuse a ride with any person who is or has been drinking.* It's your life.

A girl especially must often face a hard decision. Does she get into a car with a guy she's wanted to date for some time when it's apparent he's half in the bag? Are there any sensible alternatives for her, short of refusing to go out with him? If she has a license, she might offer to drive. Or she might suggest they take a cab, even offering to pay part of the fare. If her date is belligerent and unreasonable early in the evening, she can bet he's going to get worse with more to drink. Saying no may be hard to do, but an evening at home is preferable to a disaster on the highway.

Note to parents: This is a time you can step in. Many young girls who don't have problems with alcohol secretly hope that their parents will make this kind of decision for them, that their daughter is not allowed to go out with anyone who has been drinking. This takes the girl off the hook. So what if the parent seems like an ogre to the boy in question? Such a judgment, based on factual data, may even help the boy take a look at his drinking.

What do you do if a friend is heavily into mixing drugs?

This is a time when a young person can demonstrate the true meaning of friendship—looking out for another's best interests, especially when there is an imminent threat to that other's health. Anyone, young or old, who is a polydrug abuser, who mixes pills (like Seconal or tranquilizers) and alcohol, is definitely in danger. Combining certain drugs can cause the effects of the drugs taken together to be greater than the sum of the effects if they are taken separately. This phenomenon is known as drug synergism and can be fatal, since a person becomes increasingly toxic from residual drug build-up in the system. The person, in effect, can overdose without meaning to, or get so depressed he or she has to cheer up to commit suicide!

Discussing these facts with your friend is a true act of friendship. The information always means more to a young person if it comes from someone the same age. In my own case, I still remember those who were courageous enough to be honest with me, to risk my disapproval by telling me I was doing myself in. Now, several years later, I can't even recall the names of those "friends" who stood by and watched, or even encouraged me, as I drank my life away.

If the young drug abuser won't listen to your warnings, you could have a private and discreet conversation with his or her parents. This is a time when "narcing" could save a life! Parents are entitled to know if their child or adolescent is a polydrug abuser. The kid needs help—and the quicker the better.

How to stay away from that first drink
(the one that leads to all the others)

One of the surest way to stay sober is to hang out with other kids who don't drink. Let's face it, we become like the people we are with. There is a saying: "Don't tell me *what* you know, tell me *who* you know, and I'll tell you *what* you know." If you're trying to stay sober, it makes no sense to be running around with kids who are abusing alcohol. There is plenty of common ground for friendship among sober alcoholics (try a young AA group), as people have a way of relating better when they are not fuzzed out from alcohol.

If you are addictive, any amount or form of alcohol—or any other mood-altering drug—can set off the craving to drink again. Read labels before you take things like cough medicine or mineral supplements. Nyquil and Geritol, for instance, contain more alcohol than most beers or wines. People can delude themselves into thinking they are abstaining while going through cases of "medicine" containing twenty-five percent or more alcohol. One youngster we saw had hijacked some Nyquil from a drugstore loading dock. In a three-day period he drank over a hundred dollars worth of the stuff. His parents caught on when his tongue and eyeballs turned green.

A drug is a drug is a drug

If you have had trouble with alcohol and stopped using it, you've probably wondered about smoking a social joint, dropping an occasional red (Seconal) or Quaalude to mellow out, sniffing some cocaine to get you up for a concert. After all, they don't contain alcohol.

You're right! None of the above contain alcohol. But, like alcohol, barbiturates, cocaine, tranquilizers and pot are drugs. And if you've abused alcohol, you can almost bet the rent you'll have problems with other drugs. For the addictive person, *any* type or shape of a mood-changing chemical spells trouble. Legions of people have stopped using one drug, only to move to another—hopefully safer—drug, with disastrous results. Not only did they get hooked on the "safer" drug, but most eventually went back to the first troublemaking drug with an even greater vengeance. Once a person abuses one drug, there are strong indications he or she will be unable to use any mood-altering chemical in moderation. A study of a group of addicts in British Columbia who stopped using heroin but decided they could drink safely helps prove this point. Almost without exception, they became out-of-control drinkers, and most returned to using heroin. Only those that remained completely drug-free of all drugs were able to stay away from heroin and alcohol.

Isn't pot supposed to be safe?

No one yet has conclusively proved that marijuana is *either* harmful or safe. I heard one juvenile court judge make the statement that a person stands as much chance of choking to death on the Baggie it's carried in than getting hurt by a marijuana cigarette.

That may be so, though it has no scientific basis. A non-addictive person probably would not have trouble smoking an occasional joint. Except for the fact that pot is illegal in most states and alcohol for adults is not, the only-now-and-then marijuana smoker can be likened to the one-beer-before-dinner drinker.

But for the pilot-light people, those inclined to addiction, it's a different ball game. The comment of a boy in our group is a good indication of how it is with addictive ones. Referring to smoking dope after he had given up drinking, he said, "It got to where all I wanted to do is smoke it, morning, noon and night. Almost all of my energy was going into buying it, smoking it, earning the money to buy it, stealing so I could buy it, or hiding my stash from my parents and probation officer. Near the end of my dope smoking, I was trying to figure out how to roll a joint as big as a torpedo and put it on training wheels. That way I could move it around my house and toke on it all day. It was then I thought maybe I wasn't a 'social dope smoker.'"

Switching to another mood-changer, as from alcohol to marijuana, just trades one addiction for another. It's all the same disease, a dependency on chemicals. For an addictive person, a drug is a drug is a drug.

Can meditation help a young person stay away from alcohol?

This is a question that we — and many others in the field — are actively investigating.

As a young person begins abusing alcohol and other drugs, the tendency is to react inappropriately to situations in life, *whether or not he or she is directly under the drug's influence*. Responsibility for his or her actions is transferred to others—parents, school officials, juvenile justice authorities. In other words, continuous abuse of alcohol or any other chemical substance prevents a young person from developing skills necessary to function positively at home, in school or in the community. The more out-of-control the youth becomes, the greater the erosion of self-confidence, and the greater the need to escape by means of alcohol or other drugs.

Then, as a poor self-image becomes more solidly reinforced by behavior resulting from the drug abuse, anxiety, gloomy projection and inner tension build. This further alienates the young alcoholic from a society he or she already sees as hostile and threatening. As the youth's drinking moves into addiction, he or she continually makes poor life-affecting decisions.

Bad judgments lower self-image and result in further need for drug "highs" in order to blot out the bad feelings.

Traditional from-the-outside-in therapeutic models for the young alcoholic have had only moderate success. High anxiety and low self-esteem tend to limit the effectiveness of this kind of treatment. Lasting healing must come from within—freedom is an inside job. Meditation is one of the tools used to lower anxiety, reduce hostility and improve individual self-concepts.

In studies with habitual users of alcohol and marijuana, regular practice of meditation has been shown to help remove the craving for drugs and increase self-esteem. Drs. Robert Wallace and Herbert Benson have conducted demonstration projects indicating that seventy-five percent of habitual marijuana smokers ceased using the drug completely after meditating regularly for twelve months. Of those who quit smoking pot, the majority stated that the drug had lost its appeal and had become less pleasurable.

In a survey conducted by Drs. Lavely and Jaffe regarding the frequency of alcohol use among individuals practicing meditation, forty percent of the subjects who had meditated regularly for more than two years reported discontinuation of the alcohol use within the first six months. After twenty-five to twenty-nine months of meditation, this figure increased to sixty percent. Though conducted with users, not abusers, the authors suggest that meditation could be an effective tool to combat alcohol abuse.

Even in the most forbidding environment, such as a prison, meditation has been used as a therapeutic tool in working with inmates, ninety percent of whom are abusers of alcohol and other drugs. *The Meditation Handbook* by Tom Alibrandi (Major Books) summarizes the results:

"Using the State Trait Inventory as a testing tool, tension rates decreased markedly among most meditating inmates.

These inmates also showed appreciably less anxiety than their non-meditating counterparts. In addition to this drop in anxiety rate, they showed a sharp decrease in *boredom, resentment against authority, depression and drug abuse.* * Even more interesting, while remaining in the same hostile environment, their physical health, emotional stability and ability to get along with others (both inmates and prison officials) all improved sharply.

"Meditation appears to increase an inmate's *self-esteem, open-mindedness and hope for the future.* * He begins to feel better about himself and his chances to live in society without breaking the law. The states of California, Texas, Minnesota and Connecticut are currently instituting programs to make meditation courses voluntarily available to inmates."

Boredom. Resentment against authority. Depression. Drug abuse. These are familiar terms to anyone working with the adolescent alcohol abuser. Anything that helps a young alcoholic feel better about himself lessens the value of the drinking experience to that youngster.

Alcoholics Anonymous, in the Eleventh Step of its recovery program, invites the alcoholic to seek through prayer and meditation to improve one's conscious contact with God . . . But, as in AA's program for recovery, there are certain suggested actions that precede the meditative experience. These include stopping drinking and cleaning up the messes caused by one's alcohol abuse. Once these steps are taken, the meditator's ability to go within is enhanced.

The principle, which echoes the AA steps of recovery, is that for the alcoholic it is nearly impossible to improve in any way until he or she deals with the drinking. Once abstinent, the recovering person can begin to clear away past wreckage.

To enjoy the maximum benefits of meditation, the young alcohol abuser should stop drinking. Although if the youth attempts to meditate while still drinking, the overall stress

---

*My emphasis.

level and the need for alcohol may be reduced. At the very least, the meditative experience offers an alternate method of getting "high." It is an unusual youngster, however, who will, unsupervised, continue meditating regularly while also drinking. Regular meditation can take twelve to eighteen months before the stress level is lowered to the point where drinking is no longer of value. Unless they stop drinking, most young alcohol-abusers stop meditating before the long-term benefits of meditation can help reduce their need to drink.

At present we in the Orange County youth alcoholism program hope to investigate the effects of regular meditation on young alcohol-abusers who continue to drink. They will be asked to come in once a week for a meditation class. They will also be required to keep individual blind diaries to record frequency of meditation and how it appears to affect the quality of their lives.

We intend to answer the questions: "Does regular meditation reduce the need for alcohol among teen and preteen abusers?" "Does the young alcoholic who meditates regularly get to school more often, follow parents' instructions better, enjoy improved relationships with friends, and become motivated to get a job?" "Will abuse of alcohol diminish the ability and desire to meditate?"

The control group of meditating alcohol-abusers will be compared—using their checklist diaries—with non-meditating teen and preteen alcohol-abusers who have received the same alcohol-awareness information without the meditation instruction.

Several alcoholism centers around the country are now incorporating yoga and other systems of meditation in their youth chemical dependency programs. Facilities like St. Mary's Hospital youth unit, Pharm House and Shanti House in Minneapolis and New Connection in St. Paul (Minnesota) schedule regular yoga exercise and meditation.

There are other self-awareness tools a young alcoholic can use. Biofeedback, the science of monitoring one's stress level, has been shown to increase an alcoholic's ability to relax. More investigation needs to be done with young alcohol-abusers and biofeedback.

Young alcoholics have to learn that *it is not what happens to them but their attitudes toward what happens that is important.* Youngsters who are locked up in juvenile hall usually are there because they reacted inappropriately to some situation in their lives. If a biofeedback machine could aid such youths in measuring their moods, it might help them adjust their attitudes toward their environment and lower their overall stress. But biofeedback, along with other self-improvement tools, only works when the young person is willing to use these tools to effect a change. Young alcohol-abusers develop new attitudes only when they get sick of the consequences of the old ones.

In the same way, alcoholism treatment programs obviously are most effective when the alcohol-abuser decides he or she has a problem and stops drinking. They are practically useless unless the young alcoholic faces his or her drinking problem. Without the admission that there is, indeed, a problem and the commitment to do something about it, the young person could just as well get drunk (somehow) in a closed-care facility. And some of them do.

It all comes back to the necessity of accepting alcohol as the real troublemaker, and therefore becoming willing to get —and stay—sober.

11

How One Program Works

"We didn't realize our son was drinking so much until he got arrested and sobered up in jail. We apparently hadn't seen him straight for years," said the mother and father of a fourteen-year-old boy, upon joining our parents' workshop on alcoholism.

☆ ☆ ☆

"My qualification for doing this work is that I was the kind of a kid my parents didn't want me associating with." Jim Gilmore, juvenile counselor.

☆ ☆ ☆

John, age seventeen, announced one night in our group that he was paying back a debt to his father.

I asked, "Why do you owe him the money?"

"I was driving his car one night and the radiator got broken."

Now that sounds reasonable. But John was attending our group because he had a problem with alcohol, not because he had trouble with radiators.

So I asked, "How did the radiator 'get broken'?"

"When I hit the tree," John answered, with a look of surprise that indicated he had discovered something new.

The group roared. This is a perfect example of how a young alcoholic blocks out certain facts and bends the story to fit his or her own self-image. The fact that he had hit the tree while drunk had become irrelevant to him, therefore not important enough to store away for future reference. Why? Because John maintained he didn't have a drinking problem; his problem was his parents—especially his father, for insisting that John pay for the consequences of his drinking. Young alcoholics see things as they aren't. And it practically takes one to know one.

Although the young alcoholic may be confronted by a parent, teacher, minister, priest, rabbi, doctor or alcoholism counselor, until he or she accepts the data and admits the problem, chances are slim for recovery. That data—how others close to the young person see the effects of his or her drinking—is extremely important; but the ultimate admission must come from the problem drinker.

The significance of this realization is stated in the First Step of the Alcoholics Anonymous program for recovery: "We admitted we were powerless over alcohol—that our lives had become unmanageable."

Most treatment programs that are successful start with this First Step of AA. A young alcoholic must be shown that his or her life has become unmanageable, that there is something seriously wrong with the way he or she drinks. He or she must understand that alcohol is consistently and adversely affecting one or more areas of life.

This is what we attempt to do through alcoholism counseling in our youth program at the Alcoholism Council of Orange County.

We should mention, first, that we, as counselors, never label a young person an alcoholic, even though most of those we see have reached alcoholic proportions in their drinking. The admission must come from them. We just remind them that they weren't sent to an alcohol abuse program for singing too loud in church.

Our main effort is teaching youngsters how to do better, and therefore feel better, about themselves. A kid doesn't choose the hell that comes through abusing alcohol. If a young person is alcoholic and continues to drink, he or she is nearly powerless to change the course of his/her life. Although many think they can "quit any time" by changing their drinking habits or their brands of alcohol or the amounts they plan to consume, unless they discover for themselves this "powerlessness" they stay on the not-so-merry-go-round of alcohol abuse.

Even though they may try to do better—follow parents' instructions, make it to school, get off probation, get a job, or any of the other things we suggest—alcohol keeps getting in the way. When a youngster tries and fails, this isolates his/her drinking problem and points to it as the real culprit, the underlying cause of the trouble.

About twenty percent—maybe two out of ten—are able to turn their lives around *while* attending our program. For the others, some very potent and important timed-release information has been absorbed. Young people sometimes come back to us a year after they have left our program to report that they had finally faced their drinking problems. Some had joined AA. Some had stopped drinking on their own or cut down on their drinking dramatically.

Those who have been able to cut down on their drinking generally are divided into two categories: non-alcoholics, who, after an isolated drinking incident, have begun drinking without consequence; and booze-fighters. Booze-fighters are young drinkers who have cut back their drinking through sheer determination and all-out war with themselves. They

111

have managed to improve their lives by changing their drinking style, drinking only at home, refusing to drive after drinking, avoiding getting caught. But for the addictive drinker, the pilot-light person, the constant battle against problem drinking and its consequences continues to give alcohol the starring role in his life. Because booze-fighters do not really change their lifestyles other than to set limits on their drinking, they are prone to fall back into old habit patterns. Their craving for relief from psychic and social pain sooner or later overpowers any self-imposed drinking restrictions. With most booze-fighters, drinking will again reach problem proportions and will have to be reckoned with. Hopefully, they will then recall some of the tools they have heard about in our group or others like it.

In our group, we have a saying, "What goes around, comes around." Meaning that any young person, through the decisions he or she makes, has a lot to say about what happens to him or her. We work toward getting young alcohol abusers to assume responsibility for what happens to them as a result of their drinking. They do not need a place to dump garbage, where they can lay blame on parents, teachers, probation officer, police officers or society as a whole. They need to learn to effect their own solutions. Blaming others for their setbacks only fogs the issue.

We encourage them to get back into school, cooperate with probation officers, stay out of trouble in the community and follow parents' instructions.

But, again, alcohol-abusing youths who try to clean up their wreckage while continuing to drink just make a new trail of rubble faster than they can pick up the old messes.

Only after quitting drinking for a time do these chronic alcohol abusers make headway with their clean-up operations.

Once sober, they begin seeing themselves in a different light—facing things maybe for the first time ever. They begin to have confidence in themselves. After learning that it is not necessary to be "victims," that people are not really out to get them, the environment seems less threatening.

Two things happen: The young people begin to recognize, through their own experiences, that they and alcohol are dangerous combinations. Their improved self-image—which come from becoming more responsible in all areas—makes life less painful and reduces the need for a chemical vacation.

Even if they slip and start drinking and getting into trouble again, they have at least discovered an inner truth that tells them that, yes, they *can* make it. They have proved that they can.

The youngsters who have been in our group for two to three months (we ask the courts for a three-month commitment) are almost always a positive influence on newer members. Many have tried our system and seen how their drinking interferes with their ability to do better. They help the newer members separate what they *think* others are doing to them from what they are actually doing to themselves.

Most of what is accomplished in our groups is through this kind of positive peer pressure, or peer modeling, by kids who have admitted they were powerless over alcohol and have attained sobriety. They are an influence which is not to be found on the streets, where old friends and drinking partners are still abusing alcohol and encouraging others to do the same.

Our volunteer counselors are recovering chemically dependent people—alcoholics and other drug addicts—who have learned to live creatively without the use of mood-changing chemicals of any kind, including marijuana.

About marijuana—it is our opinion (and many chemical dependency authorities agree) that when an alcoholic, young or old, stops drinking but still smokes pot, he or she is really smoking the booze. One chemical has been substituted for another. A mood-changer is a mood-changer, whether it is drunk, smoked, shot into the system or swallowed in the form of a pill. Any child or adolescent who opts for a chemical, rather than walking through life's problems as they come, has great difficulty growing up into a mature human being. He or she remains stunted emotionally, spiritually, morally and even intellectually. Based on our experience, anyone who substitutes another chemical for one that has been a troublemaker eventually begins abusing the new drug, or else returns to the original problem drug. Until he or she takes a look inward, turns around habit patterns that feed his or her addictive personality and examines the ways he or she relates to people, places and things, there is no breaking the destructive cycle.

In our program, we insist that those who work with young alcoholics be committed to living chemically free, experiencing life's ups and downs without mood-altering chemicals of any kind. (We do not attempt to argue about the relative destructiveness of the various drugs, including alcohol, or about the legalization of marijuana. Our job is to offer alternative lifestyles and behaviors to kids with histories of alcohol and polydrug abuse.)

Our volunteer counselors range in age from fourteen to twenty-one. Now sober, they exemplify a previously unknown choice to the problem drinker—a way of living and enjoying life free of chemicals. Sharing their experiences helps strip away that common excuse for prolonging drinking, "Everyone my age drinks."

A father in our parents' group, an alcoholic himself, offered this classic statement, referring to the unlikelihood that his son could be an alcoholic, "I spilled more than he ever drank."

One of our volunteer counselors, a fifteen-year-old boy, sober for nine months, replied, "If you hadn't spilled so much, maybe you would have gotten sober at my age."

When a young drinker snivels and bad-mouths everything and everyone around him or her as the cause of all problems, these sober peers will pick it up immediately and point out that the one common denominator in the complaining kid's difficulties is the kid himself. The other is alcohol. Eliminate the drinking, and the young person stands a good chance of avoiding the hassles with the law, the school and parents. When the message comes from someone the same age as the problem drinker—who has been there, too—it's pretty hard to ignore.

Any kind of therapy or treatment for the young alcoholic is minimally effective unless parents are also involved. The kid-fix-it-shop approach—mom and dad drop off their alcoholic-abusing young one for a carburetor tuning or a tire patch and pick the youngster up all fixed—is a myth. The entire family needs a healing experience.

At this initial stage of therapy, when the young drinkers may not have made the decision of abstinence, we have found that the best method of helping both parents and youngsters is in separate group settings. (We are aware of residential treatment programs which include parents-children groups, along with separate groups for children and parents. These joint sessions seem to work more successfully in residential treatment, with young people who are free of chemicals.)

At this early stage, confrontive-type therapy between parents and young alcoholics can muddy the issue, even give the teen or preteen more reason to drink.

We try to diffuse the resentment between parent and child by helping parents back away from their child's behavior. A child-parent forum can be a replay of what's been going on at home for years. If it had worked there, we probably wouldn't be seeing them at all. Healthy, mature and non-alcoholic youngsters communicate well with parents. Alcoholic youngsters don't.

By this time parents have found that it is useless to argue with an alcoholic child. Even the so-called heart-to-heart talks have become favorite game-playgrounds for young alcohol abusers. With promises and proclamations, the youth sets up parents to get just what he or she wants—like less stringent rules about hours or use of the family car—while having not the slightest intention of following through on his/her end.

Young alcoholics are masters at confusing the issues with words. And a parent may discover that what started out as a perfectly viable parental plan for "fixing" the child's problems has been so twisted out of shape as to be unrecognizable.

After the young person makes a decision about drinking, communication can take place. Until then, it's liable to be a con job, with both sides guilty of vacant promises and threats, bribery and manipulation.

Parents hope for something like: "Gee, Dad, I never looked at it that way. You're right. My drinking is totally out of control. I'm quitting." This approach looks terrific on family TV shows, but it seldom works that way. A child or adolescent who stops drinking because of a conversation with parents probably is not dependent on alcohol. Alcoholic behavior comes from such a depth that simple conversations don't fix it.

What we do ask is that parents set firm guidelines of behavior around the house—not just talk about them. Conversation without action sets up a smokescreen. Keep things simple. Set limits or boundaries. Expect them to be respected. Then back off (if you can) from the kid's behavior.

When the young person does not operate within these boundaries—and alcohol-abusing kids rarely can—the parent then deals with the behavior with appropriate consequences.

This does not mean yelling, "punching the kid's lights out" or even discussing it. Screaming at a sick person does no good. Nor does roughing up. The spare-the-rod-spoil-the-child method may have worked when the child was five years old (which I seriously question), but cuffing around an adolescent problem drinker only teaches one to react to frustration with violence.

Take action. And let the punishment fit the crime. For instance, if your youngster is having trouble getting home on time, you don't take away the stereo or television privileges; save those for when he or she abuses the stereo or the television agreements. Instead, when your child comes in after your curfew, without commercials, editorials or commentaries ("Why were you late?" "Where have you been?" "Have you been drinking again?"), you dock the youngster the next time he or she wants out—roughly equal to the time he or she was late.

If your child laughs at you and comes home late again, he or she may be docked once more, or even grounded until further notice. Then if he or she vanishes out of the bedroom window, increase the severity of the punishment, even though it may lead to a court petition of incorrigibility. Your child is telling you—by behaving this way—that he or she needs help. The out-of-control drinking behavior may earn the youngster a probation officer, who can help the child get on top of the problem and add muscle so you may regain control of your household.

This kind of discipline ("discipline" stems from the Greek word "to teach") demonstrates that certain actions beget certain consequences. There are logical sequences in "going down the tubes" due to alcoholic behavior, and nobody is plotting against the youth. The alcohol-abusing youngster learns that it is up to him or her to straighten out the messes.

One of the most crucial areas for parental limits has to do with driving an automobile. Drinking and driving spell irresponsibility, so don't give an alcohol-abusing child permission to take your car. Anyone who drinks and drives has a 4,000-pound lethal weapon—one that has caused more death and carnage than the entire struggle in Viet Nam.

The young drinker who hot-wires the car and takes it without permission is committing a grand theft. If the drunken youth is arrested for drunk driving (DWI), it's his/her responsibility to pay the fine and the lawyer's fees and repairs to property. If the youth is a minor dependent and does not have the necessary funds, you, as parents, will have to pay. But let your adolescent know that he or she owes it to you — and collect! It's not *your* debt.

By issuing specific instructions and guidelines, you are raising his or her "bottom," allowing the young alcohol abuser to squirm, to be uncomfortable with his or her drinking consequences. You are letting your girl or boy worry about the problem, placing the responsibility where it belongs — on the shoulders of the young drinker.

If the parent backs off and deals only with the youngster's behavior, the young alcohol abuser is no longer protected. And protected drunks, young or old, have a way of getting worse. (If the young alcoholics worried a tenth as much as their parents do, they would probably be sober.)

We think it is sad when a parent, in an effort to help a child, hides him or her from the system. Many times we have seen this parental unwillingness to face reality just postpone the young person's day of reckoning and prolong the agony. Prisons are full of men and women who never had the chance as children to face themselves and take responsibility for their actions.

A parent, by "letting go," is not exhibiting a lack of love. On the contrary, it is the highest form of love. "Tough love" means letting your youngster learn from experience, allowing the effects of alcohol abuse to be unpleasant and frequent enough so that the drinking experience decreases in value.

When parents wade into the muck themselves, by screaming, arguing, becoming physically violent, the youngster begins to see the parents, rather than alcohol, as the number one problem.

Parents should let community authorities handle any misbehavior outside their own front door. If your youngsters have run-ins with the police because of drinking, allow them to make it right, and try not to blow a gasket because they get in trouble. View an alcohol-abusing youth's experiences with the law in the same context as the crime-and-punishment sequences in your own house. Give him or her the chance to learn from what happens.

If your alcohol-abusing child does land on probation, work closely with the officer assigned to the case. That is what those officers are for, to help you and your youngster. In essence, the court has said that your child is a ward of the court, who is only allowed to live in your house *as long as he or she follows the rules.*

If the young person violates any of the terms of the probation, first give him or her the chance to call the probation officer. This is not "narcing." If you give young people the chance to right their own wrongs and alert the probation officers to information they are entitled to know, you are getting across an important message. Everyone makes mistakes. That's why they put erasers on pencils. This kind of message should be consistent through the system — whether through parents, probation officers, work programs, residential treatment or closed care or juvenile camp. Thus, step by step, the alcoholic youngster is shown that out-of-control drinking behavior is unacceptable at home and in the community.

All the while, the alcoholism counselor is pointing out to these youngsters that what is happening to them is not an accident or a conspiracy against them, but the logical and predictable consequence of drinking behavior. This is not easy, because a young alcoholic usually believes sincerely that the juvenile justice system, police and society in general are unreasonable monsters that single out and arrest youths for behaviors that adults get away with. ("Things are slow in juvenile hall tonight; let's bust Johnny or Susie!")

Counselors help the young alcoholic see that they cannot predict or control their actions when they drink, that alcohol itself has become an "authority," a dictator with its *own* rules of behavior, a lot more demanding a taskmaster than parents, teachers or police.

This information is most effective when it comes from an alcoholism counselor or the group, rather than parents.

We also suggest that the parents instruct the youngster to get a job (don't offer this as an option—require it) by a certain date. Taking on a job helps the young alcoholic develop some good feelings about self, become more self-sufficient and start amassing a few dollars to pay debts—including those to parents. Even if some of the earnings go for alcohol, the young person has become partly responsible for his or her financial obligations, and will learn just how much muscle on the job it takes to buy a bottle.

Working takes a young alcoholic out of the ranks of the protected drunks. He or she has to make it to work on time and perform on the job—in spite of hangovers, an upset stomach, diarrhea or raw nerve endings. The do-nothing time is reduced. (People don't feel good about themselves if all they do is lie in front of the television, changing channels with their toes.)

The importance of a job for the young alcoholic really is that he or she moves into another area where drinking can be isolated as the problem. It is not easy to keep a job if you show up late or listless from an alcoholically negative attitude. Chances are good he or she will be fired, or at least reprimanded, probably not once, but over and over again in a succession of job failures. This way, drinking is shown to interfere seriously with the young person's ability to function on the job. Pressure from employers and fellow employees has long been recognized as a good way for an individual, of any age, to begin to analyze his or her drinking patterns.

By allowing your young alcoholic the honor of blowing a few jobs because of drinking-related unproductiveness, you are helping to point out the need for change—and not an artificial one. You can accelerate this need by not covering for him or her, financially or any other way. Letting your child under eighteen learn how the real world works might spare some later, more serious consequences of alcohol abuse. It is a great deal more tragic when an adult with two or three dependent children gets fired for drinking.

This, then, is basically the way our program works in Orange County. To sum up, we attempt to show the youngster that what is happening to him or her is a direct result of drinking. We do this through counseling and the group process. The value of the examples offered by young, recovering chemically dependent counselors—and by those like Carla, Pat, Jack, Jana and Denny who have found comfortable sobriety—cannot be overemphasized. We try to work out with the young drinker ways to better her or his life by assuming for self-responsibility. In separate groups, we help parents understand and make use of the juvenile justice system, how to let the system work with them in dealing with their alcoholic youngsters. With this kind of confidence, they can begin to back away from their children's poor behavior and allow those young people to handle their own "logical consequences"—and face themselves.

12

Strong Feelings, Strong Opinions

"Physicians who are familiar with alcoholism agree there is no such thing as making a normal drinker out of an alcoholic." *Alcoholics Anonymous*, second edition.

☆　☆　☆

"If you wanted to feel the same way all the time, you should have been born a rock." Jack, a fifteen year old sober alcoholic.

☆　☆　☆

Sharon

Just a month before beginning to work on this book, I was called to the hospital by the mother of a fifteen-year-old girl we had seen earlier in the year. The girl, Sharon, was in intensive care. She had overdosed and was not expected to live. The drug was alcohol.

The last time I had seen Sharon was ten months earlier on her final night in our group, the night her mother advised us she no longer could drive her daughter to counseling. She had paid a fine, in lieu of her daughter's attending six months of weekly sessions in our program. Sharon really didn't want to come anyway; she didn't feel that alcohol was her problem.

Her mother had become angry when I had suggested her daughter might be an alcoholic and things could get worse. "Alcoholic? Sharon drinks some beer, like every other kid. She just needs to be more careful when she drinks."

In the hospital waiting room, I asked Sharon's mother what had happened.

"She started drinking bad. It happened before I realized."

Sharon died that afternoon, having downed enough of the depressant drug, alcohol, to put her vital functions to sleep—permanently. Even if she had lived, the doctor said, she had suffered massive brain damage from lack of oxygen when the alcohol had caused her to stop breathing. The doctor consoled Sharon's mother by saying that it was highly unusual for someone to die from an overdose of alcohol. It was more common, he said, to treat youngsters for alcohol-related injuries and illnesses—occurrences, he admitted, that he was seeing more and more frequently.

☆　☆　☆

Anyone who works with adolescent alcoholics tends to be somewhat categorical. Strong feelings resolve into strong opinions. In looking back over this book, I find that I have been highly opinionated in places. But I hope I have avoided being preachy. No one is an infallible authority on youth alcoholism. We are just beginning to understand the effects of alcohol on children and adolescents. But there are some hopeful beginnings.

This kind of work—which also involves sifting facts from myths, notions and delusions—makes one intolerant of our chemically oriented society's inclination to gloss over obvious problems and potential tragedies. Working with alcoholic youngsters solidifies one's convictions about the power of addiction and the requirement of absolute abstinence if the young problem drinker is to tap life's potential. So many of them don't make it, get dusted, as they say, like the seventeen-year-old boy in our group who was killed in a car wreck. He had been drinking when it happened; his blood-alcohol count was .23.

Less dramatic examples are the legions of kids in this country who won't face the fact that alcohol is getting in the way of self-fulfillment. These almost always are bright and creative youngsters, who, because of abusing alcohol, become intellectually, emotionally and spiritually bankrupt —along with making wrecks of themselves physically. Because they are alcoholics, they are menaces to themselves, their parents, their community and their world.

You feel strongly when you walk into a juvenile detention facility and see the familiar faces, the half-scared, half-arrogant looks of adolescents you have worked with, kids who still believe the system is out to get them. It's those kids against the world. And their energy is alcohol.

A part of you hopes anxiously that these young ones will finally see how it works, that it is alcohol—not a probation officer, judge, parent or arresting officer—that is stealing their freedom. Another part of you understands the horrible reality that only one out of thirty-six alcoholics finds sobriety. The rest end up in institutions, hospitals or cemeteries.

It's tough to remain calm and neutral when school board officials turn away from the problem of alcoholism among students in their districts and are unwilling to admit a problem that seems about as subtle as a train wreck.

Public disinclination to accept facts is born of a lack of information, special economic or political interests, and an overriding acceptance of alcohol, the "proper" drug of our society. This attitude among some school personnel and board members, as well as among county and state substance abuse officials, often blocks the instituting of effective programs in schools that desperately need them.

As a counselor I get angry when I read in an NIAAA-approved book that young people's groups of Alcoholics Anonymous are growing at a "frightening" rate. This is an ill-chosen combination of words. It is not the increasing number of youth AA groups that is "frightening," but the ballooning statistics which show how many young alcohol abusers are NOT getting help for their problems. There is nothing disgraceful about a youngster admitting he or she has an alcohol problem and doing something about it.

I am disheartened when parents, either because of mis-information or their own drinking problems, deny that their children might be drinking out of control—even when the signs have been unmistakable for months or possibly years. Then, because of the stigma attached to alcohol problems, they subtly or blatantly discourage a problem-drinking youngster from seeking treatment.

Adults who refuse to learn more about preteen and teen drug abuse, especially alcoholism, are denying that the problem exists. Failure to respond to the obvious is to accept and suffer myriad consequences and tragedies of youth alcoholism—emotionally sick and broken families; school truancy and lower standards of education; high medical and welfare costs; increased expense for law enforcement and juvenile detention facilities; assaults and other criminal offenses; shoplifting losses; accidents, including automobile injuries and deaths. The list could go on forever. As the attendant costs of alcoholism climb measurably, the cost in human lives and despair can't even be approximated.

The United States Department of Health, Education and Welfare (HEW), urging adoption of a National Teenage Alcohol Education Program, said, in their December 1976 request for funding to the Senate Appropriations Subcommittee:

"It should be stated at the outset that alcohol abuse and its consequences represent a very real and complex danger to the youth of this country, as well as to our society as a whole. This problem did not evolve overnight and it will require a long-term and serious commitment by all segments of society —government, industry, the community, schools, the media, the family—to affect the problem in a significant way."

We are a society that strives to demonstrate responsibility. Evidence of atrocities and denial of human rights—in our own and in other countries—rouses public outcry. When natural disaster strikes, the United States generally is the first to respond, offering free goods and services. Yet we move painfully slow to deal with a problem taking countless lives and causing untold misery right under our noses—teen and preteen alcoholism.

Only recently have studies like the one we conducted in Orange County zeroed in on the truth about youth drinking patterns.

There is a need for more studies to evaluate youth alcoholism. Standard methods of predicting and detecting youth alcohol abuse need to be developed. The value of existing youth alcoholism programs needs to be measured. Successful models of treatment in certain areas of the country need to be made available to other areas.

Separate agencies are needed to deal with chemically dependent young people. Too often, programs for young alcohol abusers have been lost or watered down within the overall maze of alcoholism education and treatment efforts. When funds are short, programs to help youthful alcohol abusers frequently are cut, and the schools are left to pick up the slack. General educational facilities simply are not able to answer the need because of budget problems of their own. Much of the best work in this field at present is done through privately funded facilities and the efforts of individuals.

School boards and school officials need to recognize the problem of youth alcoholism, a major cause of truancy in their districts. Neighborhoods need to welcome halfway houses as stabilizing influences. Chemical dependency counselors and peer groups and parent workshops should be part of every school from junior high on up. And alcohol awareness programs should be tucked into every grade school curriculum.

Alcoholism programs should be offered within all juvenile detention facilities, and long-range monitoring of the recidivism rate of those offenders who receive treatment, as opposed to those who don't, is necessary. Any alcohol-abusing youths who are able to overcome their problem and stay out of jail save taxpayers enormous amounts of money in court costs and detention facility overhead.

Initiating ways to combat youth alcohol abuse need not be left to elected or appointed officials. Armed with a perspective on current drinking problems among youth, parents can demand that programs be instituted in schools or in other community facilities. Elected school board officials are apt to respond to pressure from voters. Parents should find out what, if any, detection or interception models are being used in their school districts. After all, their children's lives are at stake.

The media must be used to counteract the "better living through chemistry" brainwashing which has taught our youth that there is a pill for every ill, that you can control your feelings, relationships, status and who-knows-what-else chemically. Public personalities—rock music idols, movie and television and sports heroes—should do their part in presenting responsible images and information.

The importance of the media was pointed out by HEW in their 1976 funding request for a National Teenage Alcohol Education Program:

"National studies show that the twelve to eighteen age group listens to radio an average of three hours and six minutes per day and that 99.4 percent of the U.S. teenage population is reached every day by radio over a seven-day week. Radio may also be the most effective and efficient media for reaching the "dropout" subpopulation, a high-risk group (for alcoholism) that will be one of the priority audiences of the national youth education strategy."

When we know that the average kid watches 22,000 hours of television by the age of eighteen, the awesome power of the media over youth becomes clear.

Courses to teach counselors to work with young alcoholics need to be instituted. Only a few colleges and universities now offer counselor training programs in youth chemical dependency. Successful treatment programs for young alcoholics and other drug abusers, where counselors can intern, are limited in number and tend to be concentrated in certain areas of the country.

Detection, interception and referral of the young alcoholic are only the beginning of a recovery process. There must be skilled people on the treatment end. If not, you have the old "all dressed up and nowhere to go" dilemma.

Again, we stress the need for young alcoholism counselors who can pass along their own joy in sobriety by sharing their own experiences of recovery and life-improving behavior. The young problem drinker then can hear, first hand, the benefits of making it to school, following parents' guidance, holding a job, staying out of trouble. These advantages are lauded, not from an adult reference point, but from a contemporary who's been there.

Conversely, anyone who is an alcohol or other drug abuser ought not to try to be a counselor for youth until his or her own problem is faced and solved. A young person will detect a practicing alcoholic in less than a minute. (People who get high have a silent language; they can spot each other a county away.) Then the counselor's advice becomes just another replay of that old adult-to-child theme: "Do as I say, not as I do."

Anyone who chooses to work with young alcoholics first needs to be convinced of who and what he or she is—and to be committed to the conviction that, for the addictive person, living chemically free is the only way.

The most effective counselor represents a way of life, a road out of the maze of dependency, without preaching or moralizing. If anyone is in the alcoholism counseling field to save souls or make notches on the gun butt for every kid saved, he or she had better find a new profession. If you take credit for the ones who make it, you also have to take blame for those who don't.

Some nonprofessionals have developed a keen knowledge of the disease as manifested in young people, mostly by learning that logic and reason and traditional psychotherapy have minimal value with an illogical, unreasonable alcoholic kid who will say anything to get out of a jam. Sometimes it takes a con artist (or ex con artist) to not get conned by one. Add to that street savvy the kind of compassion that comes through dealing with one's own alcohol or other drug problem, and you have an invaluable combination that seems to work successfully with young alcoholics.

What kinds of treatment programs—outpatient, residential, school or outside-of-school—exist for young alcoholics?

The answer is, "Not nearly enough."

Hopefully, the youngster who is abusing alcohol or other drugs can be intercepted at the family and school hassles stage, before he or she gets into more serious entanglements with police and the courts.

In that hope, a test like the At Risk Diagnostic Screening Device for preteens, developed from our Orange County survey, could be used to predict which preteens might be headed for trouble with alcohol, so that they could be given information and tools to avoid it.

As an adjunct to this test for preteens, we have designed an early interception awareness class, which offers living skills to at-risk preteens. The curriculum for this life awareness class and the screening device should be further studied for effectiveness by comparing three groups: a participating control group of at-risk preteens; at-risk preteens who are not part of the preventive counseling program; preteens in general.

Using the Youth Diagnostic Screening Device for Problem Drinkers to determine those teenagers who have reached problem levels in their drinking, we have devised a treatment program for teens. This would include peer counseling classes in school, manned by specially trained young people, close in age to the teen problem drinkers, who are themselves recovering from alcohol problems. A trained adult facilitator would be in charge. Both behavior modification tools and attitudinal information about alcohol would be part of the curriculum.

The teen problem drinkers also would be introduced to young people's AA meetings.

Parent workshops would help adults develop skills to cope with their alcohol-abusing youngsters, and to set up the framework which lets the youths see alcohol as their problem, thus saving parents from the worst of the destructive dynamics of an alcoholic family.

A method of measuring program effectiveness for teens will also be employed. Specifically, it would compare teen problem drinkers (drawn from a pool supplied by the Youth Diagnostic Screening Device for Problem Drinkers) who had been involved in this kind of program with those teen alcohol abusers *not* attending peer modeling classes and AA meetings and whose parents do *not* participate in the adult workshops.

At best, these preteen at-risk peer counseling and awareness classes and teen problem drinking peer counseling groups would raise awareness levels of potential problem drinkers and problem drinkers, so they can seek help earlier. At the least, these programs would deliver valuable information and tools for surviving in a chemically-oriented society.

Even though the young alcoholics go right out and get in trouble again, some important seeds have been planted. Like a timed-release capsule, the information often "goes off" later —in a dawning awareness or a flash of insight that it is, in fact, the abuse of the drug, alcohol, that is the real trouble-maker.

Some young people with serious drinking problems undergo strong spiritual experiences or religious conversions, cease using alcohol and dramatically improve the quality of their lives with the help of their religious fellowship—or their Higher Power, as AA calls it.

Other young alcoholics have responded to the attack therapy approach pioneered by Synanon. Or they have become involved with aversion therapy, like the programs which prescribe Antabuse, a drug which, when combined with alcohol, causes a person to become violently ill.

Often there is the parents' dilemma: Does a child need psychotherapy first and then treatment for alcoholism? Or the other way around? One professional school of thought suggests psychotherapy first, then the "folk therapy" of AA. Other strong voices in the treatment field proclaim that, until the young person is free of chemicals, there is little point in pursuing psychotherapy. Many emotional problems seem to vanish when the person stops drinking or using other drugs.

But there appears to be one certainty. Until a young alcoholic stops drinking, and, through some type of ongoing treatment program, changes her or his destructive habit patterns, he or she is prone to drink again.

Problem drinking, many believe, is the outward manifestation of deeper, underlying problems. The inability to deal with stress or disappointment, inherent dishonesty and unhealthy decision-making qualities are only a part of the make-up of a young alcoholic's personality. All of these must be dealt with in order to maintain sobriety. Since alcoholism is a disease of the whole person, a healing of the whole person is required.

Our Orange County survey points out that behavior of peers is a reliable predictor of problem drinking. In this disease, in which peer pressure is so important, peer counseling, peer modeling and peer support groups become an essential ingredient for treatment. There is some indefinable, immeasurable magic about recovery from addiction which does infect others, especially if it is exemplified in a contemporary.

The need is great for programs aimed specifically at treating today's drug addict, the young alcoholic—not programs that create a forest of desk jobs, that steep in their own bureaucratic juices, but lean and effective programs offering treatment to young alcohol abusers as symptoms first become apparent. Such early intervention programs benefit not only the young people involved, but make for healthier families, schools and communities.

We require programs first of all that isolate the alcohol-abusing youngster's drinking behavior so he or she can see it objectively, that offer tools for maintaining sobriety and for living creatively and responsibly in our world.

Should the programs designed to intercept the problem early fail—and for those alcoholic youths who don't respond to outpatient counseling—there are hospital-based and other resident treatment programs for young alcoholics.

These same elements—specially trained counselors, peer groups, AA groups and information sessions, along with some one-to-one counseling and family involvement—are present in many successful youth treatment programs.

In the area of Minneapolis and St. Paul, there are several programs for youth, providing a continuum of residential care from detoxification through primary treatment and halfway-house living, followed by aftercare programs. These, of course, require abstinence.

Some of these programs lean toward a behavior modification approach or borrow from other forms of therapy.

Some are built mainly on the premise that addiction to alcohol or other drugs is also a "disease of feelings." These children and adolescents have hidden their anger, guilt, hurt, sadness, under a suffocating blanket of alcohol and/or other drug use. They attend information lectures, peer group sessions, one-to-ones with counselors and doctors, AA meetings, and they learn to recognize and respect their own feelings—and those of other people. Parents and other family members are involved in family groups—joint sessions for parents and the now-abstaining young people, where angers and guilts and hurt generated by the alcoholic behavior come out into the open, along with a lot of underlying love and caring of parents for child, and vice versa. And the healing of the family may begin.

Yes, a person tends to develop strong feelings when working with young people whose lives are in shambles due to drinking. No matter how calloused or experienced or cool, a counselor feels more than a twinge of despair when youngsters close their minds to the realities of alcoholism. But you have to believe that your efforts are never wasted. While one young drinker is shutting you out, another in the group might be listening, identifying, silently resolving to turn things around for the better. Even the closed-minded drinkers may be absorbing what you have to say by means of some inner antennae that take in information for later recall. When they get tired of fighting their way upstream against a destructive current of alcoholism much swifter than they are strong, maybe the words of counselor and peer group will come back to them.

If only we had had the chance to follow through and reach Sharon. As I drove back to my office from the hospital the day she died, I thought about her inability to understand the nature and seriousness of the disease of alcoholism, especially how it related to herself—a fifteen-year-old girl. She simply had not been able to see herself as an alcoholic. By drinking "more sensibly" and not getting caught when she drank, she felt she could handle it.

Arriving at the offices of the Alcoholism Council of Orange County, I was greeted by one of the newer volunteer workers. Mickey, age sixteen, is an alcoholic. She had joined

AA six months before, while attending our group. Mickey, now sober for more than four months, regularly donates her Tuesday afternoons, answering phones and doing clerical work at the council office.

Mickey still attends our youth group, sharing with other young people how much better everything has been for her since she admitted she is an alcoholic and stopped drinking. Sharon and Mickey used to sit next to each other in the group when they were both newcomers.

As I said before, there is something about working with alcohol-abusing kids that makes one opinionated.

Part Two

A Survey
of Drinking Patterns
and Problem Drinking
Among Youth in Orange County

August 1976
Principal Investigator:
Tom Alibrandi
Consulting Psychologist:
Dr. Douglas K. Chalmers

Youth Services Program
Alcoholism Council of Orange County (ACOC)
2110 East First Street, Suite 115
Santa Ana, California 92705

Contents

Tables

"Our goal must be to decrease interest in, availability of, and dependency on alcohol, recognizing it as a drug and as part of the total drug scene." Joel Fort, M:D., *Alcohol: Our Biggest Drug Problem.*

☆   ☆   ☆

To help explain the implications and impact of the increase in consumption of alcohol among youth, we are including portions of the 1976 study, *Drinking Patterns and Problem Drinking Among Youth in Orange County,* conducted by the Alcoholism Council of Orange County, and made possible by a grant from the Orange County Department of Mental Health.

The survey was completed in September, 1976.

Copies may be obtained by writing the Alcoholism Council of Orange County, 2110 East First Street, Santa Ana, California 92705.

The following demographic and social profiles of Orange County are offered so that it may be compared with other counties throughout the United States. This information was gathered from a 1975 Orange County Department of Mental Health report.

Orange County adjoins Los Angeles County to the south. Included in its 1.4 million (the 1976 population was 1.7 million) inhabitants are diverse socio-economic satellites.

Approximately twelve percent of the county's population is Spanish or Black, twenty percent is foreign born and six and one-half percent of youths under eighteen fall below poverty level. The county median income is $12,245. The economic makeup of county inhabitants is as follows:

Low occupational status (laborers,
   operatives, farm and service workers,
   both male and female) ....32.46 percent

Middle occupational status (clerical and
   sales workers and crafts people,
   both male and female) ....40.19 percent

High occupational status (professional
   and technical workers, managers and
   administrators, both male and female) ....27.35 percent

The occupational status breakdown of the families of youth surveyed in Drinking Patterns and Problem Drinking Among Youth in Orange County, is as follows: blue collar, 29.5 percent; white collar, 43 percent; professional and self-employed, 27.5 percent.

There are approximately 500,000 youngsters under the age of eighteen living in Orange County, with 116,519 of those falling in the fourteen to seventeen age group. Approximately 435,000, or 87 percent, live with both parents.

The consulting psychologist, Dr. Douglas K. Chalmers, Associate Professor of Psychology at the University of California at Irvine, helped write the questionnaire, analyzed the data and prepared the findings.

A special note should be made about this report. Despite nearly complete agreement from teachers and school administrators that student drinking is an important school problem, individual school boards, with a few exceptions, were highly reluctant to approve this study of alcohol use and abuse among students tested—even though questionnaires were to be answered anonymously. And resistance to the study was not limited to the data-gathering process. The coordinator of the drug abuse prevention program for the Orange County Department of Education criticized the findings of the survey. He stated publicly (in the *Los Angeles Times*, February 11, 1977) that the youngsters, though tested anonymously, may have lied about their drinking, inflated their reports of alcohol consumption out of bravado.

Although we feel we should present this point of view, other research strongly indicates that drinkers are more apt to *understate* their rate of consumption by as much as fifty percent.

Summary

A Youth Drinking Questionnaire was devised and administered to 1,507 young people representative of Orange County elementary, junior high, high school and colleges. The mean age of the sample was 14.1 years (mean grade, 8.4). A pilot questionnaire involving 996 young people was also analyzed as a replication sample.

Two thirds of the youth had attained drinker status (see B. Incidence of Drinking and Problem Drinking), which is identical to the rate of drinking for adults in the last national sample. It is estimated that drinking rates have tripled among youth over the last years. Drinker status had been reached by about half of elementary school students, about two thirds of junior high school students, and about 85 percent of high school students. Drinker status is affected more by sociocultural factors than is the case with problem drinking.

Problem drinking was broken down into three components: drinking style, problematic consumption, and drinking consequences. Males and females differed on consumption, but did not differ reliably on style and consequences indices of problem drinking. The largest increase in pathological style occurred between elementary and junior high, and the largest increase in consumption occurred between junior high and early high school.

On parallel measures of problem drinking or alcoholism, our youth sample showed a seventeen percent incidence rate among drinkers, while the national adult sample for males only showed a sixteen percent rate. For the total youth sample, including abstainers, the rate is eleven percent. Comparable measures of heavy drinking also recorded close similarity between youth and adults. Youth appears, however, to have a larger pool of potential problem drinkers than adults. One out of four drinkers reports getting drunk at least once a month or more.

All items were assessed to determine their ability to discriminate among the problem drinking components.

Among the best discriminating nondrinking-related items are peer group behavior and drug use. A sample of the best discriminating drinking-related items are "drinking to change the way I feel," "drinking to feel more relaxed with the opposite sex," all symptomatic and binge drinking items, "drink till nothing left," all frequency of drunk occasion items and "missed school due to drinking" (see Table 9).

On the basis of the best predicting nondrinking-related items, an At-Risk Diagnostic Screening Device (Test) was devised for predicting preteens at risk of developing drinking problems. On the basis of the best predicting drinking-related items, a Problem Drinking Diagnostic Screening Device (Test) was developed to tap both *type* (style, consumption, and consequences) and *severity* (potential problem drinking, problem drinking, and alcoholism). A preliminary validation sample of teenage alcoholics was generally diagnosed correctly.

Finally, based on the present data, a peer modeling approach to prevention with preteens and intervention with youth alcohol offenders was sketched, and recommendations for its implementation were made.

A. The Youth Drinking Questionnaire

The present report will be based on the results of two independent questionnaires. The Pilot Quesionnaire was administered prior to the county contract as part of a pilot educational project of the Director of Youth Programs, ACOC. The Pilot Questionnaire served as the basis for the development of the Youth Drinking Questionnaire. The results of both questionnaires will be reported, each serving as an independent replication of the other. The Pilot Questionnaire will be referred to as Q_1, and the final Youth Drinking Questionnaire will be referred to as Q_2.

The Pilot Questionnaire (Q_1). The Pilot Questionnaire is shown in Appendix A. It contains fifty-nine questions, embracing demographic and social characteristics, alcohol consumption, drug usage, tangible drinking consequences, and pathological indicators. The drinking questions are basically an expanded version of the Twenty Questions about Alcohol for Youth (1).

Nine schools were selected for the pilot project. These schools were spread across Orange County, but were not systematically selected, except that they had contact with ACOC for the purpose of alcohol education.

The questionnaire was administered by the Director of Youth Programs, ACOC. Questions were read aloud by him in front of the class, and students responded by writing down on a blank sheet of paper their answers to each question. All response sheets were anonymous. Each questionnaire administration was accompanied by a class presentation on the topic of alcohol education. Characteristics of the sample ($N = 996$) are given in Table 1.

The Youth Drinking Questionnaire (Q_2). The Youth Drinking Questionnaire, together with the response sheet, is attached as Appendix B. Most of the questions from the Pilot Questionnaire were included, although they were refined and clarified. The items added were primarily drinking items selected for comparison with the youth drinking surveys conducted by Maddox and McCall (2), Jessor and Jessor (3), and the recent adult surveys of Cahalan and Room (4). Other items were composed as likely *a priori* predictors of problem drinking.

Due to county policy, items related to family and sex were omitted from the Youth Drinking Questionnaire.

We began with plans to interview several thousand students in twenty-seven schools in Orange County, in a design carefully stratified with respect to class and grade. However, it turned out that we had significantly underestimated the coordination effort required in relation to imposed time-lines because of the number of school districts in Orange County. The sensitivity of a study of this type dictates a great deal of advance planning and articulation with the many school superintendants and school boards. In our judgment, plans for future studies should include a coordination cycle of at least six to nine months.

Despite this, we were able to interview twelve schools that satisfied our stratified sampling design. The schools were distributed roughly equally over lower, middle and upper socio-economic regions for each of elementary, junior high, high schools and junior colleges. Our final sample size of 1,507 youths was below our initial target sample, yet sufficiently substantial for representation. Representativeness of the sample is checked by means of the data from the Pilot Questionnaire, which are intended to function primarily as a replication factor.

Questionnaires were administered to classes orally, and students responded on a prepared response sheet (Appendix B). Instructions, also shown in Appendix B, were read carefully prior to reading the questions. Four interviewers, two males and two females, previously trained in interview techniques, administered the questionnaire to roughly equal numbers of classes. Responses to both questionnaires (Q_1 and Q_2) were keypunched and entered into a series of computer programs for analysis.

Characteristics of Survey Samples. Table 1 describes the characteristics of the two survey samples administered the Pilot Questionnaire (Q_1) and the Youth Drinking Questionnaire (Q_2). Q_1 sample size is 996 students from nine schools, and Q_2 sample size is 1,507 students from twelve schools. The Q_1 sample was selected relatively randomly, while the Q_2 sample was selected from a design stratified by socioeconomic class and school grade. In comparision with the Q_2 sample, the Q_1 sample was on the average about one year older, but included seven and eight year olds. The Q_1 sample was composed of a somewhat higher percentage of boys than the Q_2 sample. Both samples were weighted more by students from white-collar families than either blue-collar or professional families. However, this weighting is more accentuated for the Q_2 sample.

Because the Q_2 sample was *a priori* stratified, it is considered to be the more representative sample. Nonetheless, both samples seem close enough in their makeup to be usefully compared and considered replications, keeping in mind the small difference between them.

Table 1. Characteristics of Survey Samples: Pilot Questionnaire (Q_1) Sample and Youth Drinking Questionnaire (Q_2) Sample.

	Q_1	Q_2
Sample size	996	1,507
Number of schools sampled	9	12
Mean age (range)	14.9 (7-21)	14.1 (9-21)
Mean grade (range)	9.5 (3-16)	8.4 (4-14)
Sex (% male)	54%	49%
Social class of family		
Blue collar	31%	28%
White collar	37%	49%
Professional and self-employed	32%	23%

Finally, we note that twelve of the 996 Q_1 youths are definite problem-drinking youths who were being treated by the Youth Program of ACOC and were administered the Pilot Questionnaire at ACOC. As they comprise about 1 percent of the sample, their effect on the results is negligible. However, their responses will be analyzed separately in a later section.

B. Incidence of Drinking and Problem Drinking

Incidence Rate of Drinker Status and Social/Attitudinal Correlates

In this section we will consider what portion of the youth in various grades actually drink at all, and what determines this incidence rate.

Definitions of incidence rate can vary widely from whether one has ever "tasted" alcohol, to whether one drinks at least once per year, to whether one considers himself or herself a "drinker." Several kinds of definitions and the associated incidence rates for the Q_1 and Q_2 samples are shown in Table 2. For these data, ninety percent had tasted alcohol, sixty-eight percent drink at least once per year, and only fifteen percent consider themselves as "persons who drink." Nonabstainers ("drinkers") for the present samples were defined as 1) those who drank with a frequency greater than "never" for the Q_1 sample (eighty-three percent), and 2) those who had "more than two or three drinks in their life" for the Q_2 sample (sixty-six percent). The latter measure of "drinkers" was that employed by Jessor and Jessor (3), and is very close to the percentage who drink "at least once a year" (sixty-eight percent).

Hence about two thirds of youth between the fourth grade and college can be considered drinkers. This rate breaks down to seventy-one percent for males and sixty-one percent for females (see Table 2).

Table 2. Incidence of Drinking, According to Various Definitions, for Q₁ and Q₂ Samples, Males and Females

	Current Samples (Age 7-21)	11th and 12th Grades* (Early 60's)	Adult Sample (1965)
Has "tasted" (Q_1)	90% (91M, 89F)	92%	
More than "never" (Q_1)	83% (86M, 81F)		
Ever had a drink — more than sip or taste (Q_2)	71% (76M, 67F)		
At least once a year (Q_2)	68% (71M, 65F)		68% (77M, 60F)
Had a drink "more than 2 or 3 times in your life" (Q_2)	66% (71M, 61F)	23%	
More than "hardly ever" (Q_1)	57% (64M, 49F)		
Had a drink "in the last week" (Q_1)	41% (47M, 33F)		
Considers self a "person who drinks" (Q_2)	16% (17M, 14F)	9% (13M, 5F)	

*Of the 11th and 12th graders (early 60's), 23% (33M, 15F) "reported that they are not abstainers and that they drink some alcoholic beverage at least occasionally."

Incidence Rate Comparisons to Earlier Studies.

As shown in Table 2, the incidence rate for persons twenty-one years and older in a national sample obtained in 1965 is sixty-eight percent (at least once per year), as determined by Cahalan, Cisin, and Crossley (5), in *American Drinking Practices.* This rate is identical to the current youth rate. The proportion of drinkers among youth in Orange County (the average being a fourteen-year-old eighth grader) in 1976, then, is the same as the proportion of adult drinkers in the population about ten years ago. In addition, whereas the adult sample consisted of seventeen percent more males than females in the current youth sample, the gap has narrowed to only six percent on the equivalent measure ("drinks at least once per year").

A more direct comparison of our Q_2 sample (mean grade, 8.4) can be made with a sample of eighth, ninth, and tenth graders (mean grade, 9) obtained by Jessor and Jessor (3) in a Rocky Mountain city in 1970, of drinkers defined by "drink more than two or three times in your life." By this measure, the Jessors obtained fifty-eight percent drinkers, compared to our rate of sixty-six percent.

Maddox and McCall (2) reported that a sample of eleventh and twelfth graders about fifteen years ago in a midwestern city had an incidence rate of twenty-three percent (thirty-three percent M, fifteen percent F), defined as drinking "at least occasionally." Roughly comparable measures of our samples (mean grade, 8 or 9) put this rate currently at between forty-one percent and sixty-eight percent (see Table 2). If we consider only eleventh and twelfth graders from the current sample (see Table 4), the incidence rate that is roughly comparable to the twenty-three percent rate of Maddox and McCall is eighty-five percent ("drinks at least once per year").

Maddox and McCall also noted that nine percent of their eleventh and twelfth graders referred to themselves as "drinkers," and discussed the meaning of this reference in the context of adolescent attitudes. Our current Q_2 sample (mean grade, 8.4) consisted of sixteen percent who referred to themselves as "drinkers," and it will be shown later that this question is one of the better predictors of problem drinking.

In summary, it is probable that drinking among youth has at least tripled over the past fifteen years, and that young people are drinking at the same rate as did adults ten years ago.

Frequency of Drinking by Grade. The incidence and frequency of drinking over the grade levels is given in Table 3 for the Q_1 sample and in Table 4 for the Q_2 sample. First, we note the differences in grade distribution for the two samples, which are given in parentheses at the bottom of the tables.

Table 3. Q_1 Sample (N = 996): Incidence and Frequency of Drinking by Grade for the Pilot Questionnaire Sample (percent).

	Grade						
	3-4	5-6	7-8	9-10	11-12	College	Overall
Never	31	26	24	11	6	9	16
Hardly ever	29	45	31	18	10	25	27
One or two times per year or holidays	35	21	23	20	4	9	17
One time per month	2	4	7	17	5	13	10
One time per week	2	1	6	9	10	11	8
Weekends	1	1	7	20	52	28	18
After school or work	0	2	1	5	13	5	4
Percent of sample	(9)	(12)	(23)	(16)	(8)	(32)	(100)

Table 4. Q_1 Sample (N = 1,507). Incidence and Frequency of Drinking by Grade for the Youth Drinking Questionnaire Sample (percent).

	Grade					
	4-6	7-8	9-10	11-12	College	Overall
Less than one time per year	55	35	19	15	14	32
One time per year	12	7	6	4	2	7
Two or three times per year	16	26	21	18	13	20
One time per month	5	11	20	19	12	13
Two or three times per month	5	12	18	21	20	14
One time per week	3	5	8	13	15	7
Two or three times per week	3	3	7	8	22	6
Every day	1	1	1	2	2	1
Percent of sample	(28)	(23)	(20)	(22)	(7)	(100)

The Q_1 sample contains a greater portion of elementary school students and a higher portion of high school and college students than the Q_2 sample. As already noted in Table 1, the Q_1 sample also contains a higher portion of males than the Q_2 sample.

As a result of these differences, the Q_1 sample has thirty percent overall who drink at least once per week, while the Q_2 sample contains only fourteen percent who drink at least once per week. In addition, different measures of frequency were obtained for the two samples. The results will be discussed with respect to the primary Q_2 sample, which gives the most direct frequency indices (Table 4).

The abstinence rate (based on "drinks less than once per year") declines rapidly from fifty-five percent for grades four to six to nineteen percent for grades nine to ten. Thus by ages fourteen and fifteen, the number of occasional drinkers is over eighty percent. Thereafter, the abstinence rate levels off at fourteen percent by college age.

Turning to drinking frequency, as shown in Table 4, the proportion who drink at least once a week is seven percent for grades four to six, nine percent for grades seven and eight, sixteen percent for grades nine and ten, twenty-three percent for grades eleven and twelve, and thirty-nine percent for college students. Just as abstinence dropped sharply between the eighth and ninth grades, so frequent drinking shows its first sharp increase during this transition. However, while the total proportion of drinkers stabilizes after this transition, the proportion of frequent drinkers continues to climb, doubling by college age.

Classification by Quantity and Frequency. The frequency classification of Table 4 was employed to match that of Cahalan and Associates (4,5) in their national adult sample. The quantity classification was formed from item 44 of Q_2 (Appendix B), which asked students to indicate their usual number of drinks per occasion. A quantity X frequency classification was developed to match as closely as possible the classification employed by Cahalan et al. (5). Our classification was probably more conservative than theirs in the heavier drinking categories, because their quantity measure was based on the "beverage drunk most often," while ours did not specify beverage.

In the youth classification, abstainers (thirty-two percent) drank less often than once a year, infrequent drinkers (twenty-seven percent) drank less than once a month but at least once a year, light drinkers (twelve percent) had no more than one or two drinks monthly or more often, moderate drinkers (thirteen percent) had three or more drinks monthly but two drinks weekly or daily, and heavy drinkers (sixteen percent) had three or more drinks weekly or daily. (The exact procedure of forming the classification is given in Appendix C.)

Table 5 displays the youth classification in comparison to the 1965 national adult sample (5). While the 1965 adult sample contained twelve percent heavy drinkers, the youth sample (mean age = 14.1) contained sixteen percent heavy drinkers. The portion of abstainers (thirty-two percent) and moderate drinkers (thirteen percent) was identical in the two samples. The main difference between the samples lies in the infrequent vs. light drinkers. Twice as many youths as adults drink less than once per month. However, if young people do drink once a month or more, they are nearly twice as likely as adults to be classified as heavy drinkers. That is, discounting abstainers and infrequent drinkers, thirty-nine percent of the youth are heavy drinkers, while only twenty-three percent of the (1965) adults are heavy drinkers.

To summarize, the primary transition for drinking incidence occurs between junior high school (grades seven and eight) and early high school (grades nine and ten). However, once drinking begins, frequency of drinking, at least weekly, increases from sixteen percent at grades nine and ten to thirty-nine percent at college. When drinking Classification is made by quantity and frequency of consumption and compared to a 1965 National Adult Sample, the youth show a higher incidence of heavy drinkers than adults, and dramatically so when considering regular users. Finally, it should be kept in mind that measures of self-reported consumption, such as those in the current survey, underestimate actual consumption by about fifty percent, especially among heavy drinkers (Pernanen, 6).

Table 5. Classification of Type of Drinker by Quantity and Frequency. Q_2 sample (mean grade = 8.4) compared to 1965 national sample of adults age 21 and over.

	Abstainers	Infrequent Drinkers	Light Drinkers	Moderate Drinkers	Heavy Drinkers
Youth Sample (1976)	32%	27%	12%	13%	16%
Adult Sample (1965)	32%	15%	28%	13%	12%

Social and Attitudinal Predictors of Drinking Incidence. Tables 6 and 7 list those variables relating to social and family background, peer group, drug usage, attitudes, school, and self-concept. In this section we will discuss these variables in relation to their ability to differentiate drinkers from nondrinkers. We will focus on the first two columns only of Tables 6 and 7.

Column 1 gives the proportion of the total sample affirming the item. Column 2 gives the product-moment correlation coefficient (r) between the item and the drinker-nondrinker classification. Thus r ranges between 0 and 1 according to the ability of the item to discriminate drinkers from nondrinkers. The remaining columns are correlation coefficients between the items and measures of problem drinking, to be discussed in detail in a later section.

All correlation coefficients given in the tables of this text are given in only tenths (1 digit) form, to facilitate reading of the tables. Any r below .20 is indicated by .1. All rs .20 and over have been rounded *down* to the lowest tenth, so that all rs listed are conservative estimates of association. (For example, correlations of .41, .45, and .49 are all rounded down to .4.)

All rs given in the tables (from .1 on up) are statistically significant at (at least) the .05 probability level. If an r was not significant, it was not included in the table. Unless an item specifies the sample (Q_1 or Q_2) from which it derives, it was actually used in both samples. If the latter is the case, then the Q_2 r is given first, with the Q_1 r in parentheses for comparison.

Proportions of the samples affirming social-family items are given in Table 6, column 1. The family items of the pilot (Q_1) sample are of particular interest. Thirty-six percent indicate that one parent drinks daily, and seventeen percent indicate a drinking problem in their household. Finally, fifty-seven percent had their first drink from their parents.

Column 2 of Table 6 indicates strength of association with drinking incidence. Age and grade are the best predictors of drinker status ($rs > .3$) followed by church attendance ($rs > -.2$). While the measures of church attendance are associated with nondrinker status, they are not associated with problem drinking among drinkers. This is also the case with parents' drinking status. Whether either parent drinks significantly predicts whether the child will be a drinker ($rs < .2$), but does not predict problem drinking among those who drink. However, whether either parent drinks daily or, in particular, has a drinking problem predicts not only drinking status of the child, but also, among drinkers, whether he is likely to have a drinking problem ($rs < .2$).

Drinker status is also weakly, but reliably, predicted by items indicating independence from the family. For one of the two samples, family size and whether the father is dead also weakly predict drinker status.

Sex is a weak predictor of drinker status, males being somewhat more likely to be drinkers than females. Socioeconomic status was not a reliable predictor for the Q_2 sample but weakly predicted drinker status for the pilot sample. Youth from professional backgrounds are less likely

Table 6. Social Differentiation among Q₁ and Q₂ Samples: Social Characteristics as Predictors of Drinking and Problem Drinking.

Correlations are given for social characteristics as predictor variables with drinker/non-drinker status, and with problem drinking among drinkers only. Where both samples are available, the Q₁ percentages and correlations are shown in parentheses. Only statistically significant correlations are given (p < .05, two-tailed).

Social Differentiations	Percent of Total Sample	Prediction of Drinking (Total Sample)	Prediction of Problem Drinking (Drinkers Only)			Overall Problems (Q₂ Only)
			Drinking Style	Consumption	Consequences	
Age (7-21)	—	.3(.4)	.3(.3)	.2(.4)	.2(.3)	.2
Grade (3-16)	—	.3(.4)	.3(.4)	.2(.4)	.2(.4)	.3
Sex (percent male)	49(54)	.1(1)	-(.1)	.1(.1)	-(.1)	.1
Has job outside home sometimes (Q₁)	79	.1	—	.1	—	
Has job outside home usually (Q₂)	47	.2	.1	.1	.1	.1
Has lived outside home	22(24)	.1(.2)	.1(.2)	.1(.2)	.1(.1)	.1
Attends church (Q₁)	54	-.2	-.1	-.1	-.1	
Attends church weekly (Q₁)	37	-.2	—	-.1	-.1	
Lives with both parents (Q₂)	77(77)	-.1(-.1)	—	-(-.1)	-(-.1)	-(-.1)
Feels that he's on his own (Q₂)	39	.1	.1	.1	.1	.1

Social Differentiations	Percent of Total Sample	Prediction of Drinking (Total Sample)	Prediction of Problem Drinking (Drinkers Only)			Overall Problems (Q2 Only)
			Drinking Style	Consumption	Consequences	
Socio-economic status (Father's work)	—	—(.1)	—	—	—	—
Blue collar	28(31)					
White collar	49(37)					
Professional or self-employed	23(32)					
Father drinks (Q1)	82	.1	—	—	—	
Mother drinks (Q1)	73	.1	—	—	—	
One parent drinks daily (Q1)	36	.1	—	.1	—	
Someone in family has drinking problem (Q1)	17	.1	.1	.1	.1	
Number of children in family	—	.1(—)	—(—)	—(—)	.1(.2)	.1
Had first drink from parents (Q1)	57	—	-.1	-.1	-.1	
Birth order	—(—)	(—)	—(—)	—(—)	—(—)	
Mother living	98(99)	—	—	—	—	
Father living	96(96)	—(.1)	—(—)	—(.1)	—(.1)	
Number of adults in residence (Q2)	—	—	—	—	—	—
Father employed (Q2)	93	—	—	—	—	—

to be abstainers (13.6 percent) than are youth from white collar backgrounds (15.2 percent.), and white collar youths are less likely to be abstainers than are blue collar youth (18.6 percent). The same trend held for the Q_2 sample, but not reliably so. However, among drinkers, socioeconomic status was not related in either sample to problem drinking.

Among the remaining predictors of drinker status, Table 7, column 2, reveals only four items with $rs > .3$. These are items in the peer group and drug use categories. The best predictor of drinker status was whether the youth had used drugs other than alcohol. The two next best predictors were whether the youth prefers to be with friends who drink and whether he favored pot over alcohol. These items also were among the strongest predictors of problem drinking. Somewhat paradoxically, those who favor pot over alcohol are more likely to be drinkers and to be problem drinkers.

The next largest group of correlations ($rs > .2$) associate drinker status with police trouble, thinking sex and drinking go together, regular cigarette smoking and considering oneself to be a "person who drinks." The latter item, however, clearly predicts problem drinking better than drinker status.

School problems and achievement orientation all weakly, but reliably, predict drinker status. The intrapersonal self-concept items did not predict drinker status, except for the depression item. The belief that drinking makes people more popular weakly predicts drinker status, and feeling uncomfortable around the opposite sex weakly predicts abstainer status.

Finally, it is of some interest to note from column 1 of Table 7 the sizable proportion of youths who think sex and drinking go together, who turn off to talks on drinking, who get depressed at times, and who feel different.

To summarize the results of Tables 6 and 7, age and grade predicted drinker status better than did sex and socioeconomic status. Cultural variables, such as church attendance and family drinking status predicted drinker status better than problem drinking. Among the strongest

Table 7. Peer Group, Drug Use, Attitudes, School Behavior, and Self-concept of Q_1 and Q_2 Samples as Predictors of Drinking and Problem Drinking.
Correlations with drinker/non-drinker status, and with problem drinking among drinkers only. When both samples are available, Q_1 percentages and correlations are given in parentheses. Only significant correlations ($p < .05$, two-tailed) are shown.

	Percent of Total Sample	Prediction of Drinking (Total Sample)	Prediction of Problem Drinking (Drinkers Only)			Overall Problems (Q_2 Only)
			Drinking Style	Consumption	Consequences	
Peer Group						
Prefers to be with friends who drink	17(19)	.2(.3)	.3(.2)	.4(.2)	.3(.1)	.3
Hangs out with kids who drink (Q_1)	53	.4	.3	.2	.3	
Drug Use						
Has used drugs	29(29)	.4(.5)	.4(.4)	.3(.5)	.3(.3)	.4
Favors pot over alcohol	21(25)	.2(.3)	.3(.3)	.2(.3)	.2(.2)	.2
Smokes cigarettes regularly (Q_2)	11	.2	.2	.2	.2	.2
Has been busted for drugs	4(6)	.1(.2)	.1(.3)	.2(.2)	.2(.3)	.2
Attitudes						
Considers self person who drinks (Q_2)	16	.2	.3	.5	.3	.4
Thinks sex and drinking go together (Q_1)	21	.2	.3	.2	.2	
Turns off to talks on drinking	30(18)	.1(−)	.1(.1)	.1(.1)	.1(.2)	.1
Believes drinking makes people more popular (Q_2)	11	.1	.1	—	.1	.1

(Table 7, *continued*)

	Percent of Total Sample	Prediction of Drinking (Total Sample)	Prediction of Problem Drinking (Drinkers Only)			Overall Problems (Q2 Only)
			Drinking Style	Consumption	Consequences	
Feels uncomfortable around opposite sex (Q2)	29	-.1	—	—	—	—
School						
Has got into trouble at school (Q2)	57	.1	.1	.1	.1	.1
Gets into school trouble often (Q2)	11	.1	.1	.1	.1	.1
Likes school most of time (Q2)	68	-.1	-.1	-.1	-.1	-.1
Gets good grades (Q2)	81	-.1	-.1	-.1	-.1	-.1
Self Concept						
Depressed at times (Q2)	59	.1	.1	—	.1	.1
Sees self as happy (Q2)	88	—	-.1	—	-.1	—
Feels different (Q2)	48	—	—	—	-.1	-.1
Likes self (Q2)	86	—	—	—	—	—
Other						
Has gotten into police trouble (Q2)	30	.2	.2	.2	.2	.3
Has heard of Alateen (Q2)	14	.1	.1	—	.1	.1
Has attended AA meeting (Q2)	4	—	—	—	.1	.1
Clearly remembers first drink (Q2)	36	.2	—	—	—	—

predictors were items relating to drug use and peer alcohol use. Intrapersonal attitudes, except for depression, uniformly failed to predict drinker status.

Problem Drinking and Social/Attitudinal Correlates

In this section, we will develop three components of problem drinking, and, on the basis of various combinations of the components, define more precisely, for present purposes, the concepts of "potential problem drinking," "problem drinking," and "alcoholism." In addition, we will compare our measures of problem drinking incidence rates to past youth and adult samples, and we will give the social/attitudinal correlates of problem drinking.

In this section, we restrict our samples to only those youth who have drinker status in the Q_1 and Q_2 samples, as defined in Table 2. As we have seen, achieving drinker status and problem drinking are discrete phenomena, whose predictor variables do not always coincide. Furthermore, including the nondrinkers in predicting problem drinking would spuriously inflate the correlation coefficients.

The Components of Problem Drinking and Their Incidence Rates. At a recent workshop on adolescent alcohol use, conferees noted that studies of young people drinking resulted in findings ranging from two percent to fifty-six percent problem drinkers (Bacon, 1976). Moreover, they made mention of published conclusions by significant national leaders that the percentage was one hundred! The differences lie clearly on the definition of the word "problem."

All definitions of problem drinking reduce to one or a combination of three considerations: (1) How much is drunk? (2) What is the manner or style of drinking? (3) What are the effects of drinking? We shall view each of these considerations as "components" or dimensions of problem drinking, and name them consumption, drinking style, and drinking consequences. Each component is broken down into three values: no problems, moderate problems, and high or severe problems. Each of the three measures is defined operationally in Appendix C, to correspond with comparable measures used in both Cahalan et al survey studies (4, 5), the more recent Harris Polls (8), and the Jessor and Jessor youth study (3).

The items comprising the drinking style component of problem drinking are listed in Table 9. They include items relating to reasons for drinking, symptomatic drinking, binge drinking, problematic intake, and belligerence. "Pathological drinking style" was indicated for the Q_2 sample if five or more of these items were affirmed.

The items making up the consumption component, listed in Table 10, are both frequency and quantity indices of alcohol intake. "Problematic consumption" was defined as having at least five drinks more often than once a month, or at least eight drinks less often.

The consequences items are shown in Table 11. They are all tangible negative consequences accruing from drinking, including home problems, school problems, social effects, physical effects, and police problems. Two or more consequences defined "severe consequences."

Table 8 displays the proportions of the Q_2 sample who fall along the three problem drinking dimensions. (Q_1 proportions, based on somewhat different component definitions, are shown in parentheses.) It is noteworthy that the Q_2 proportions differ significantly by sex only on the consumption dimension. That is, males and females do not differ on the problem drinking measures of drinking style and consequences.

Overall incidence rates for the components reveal fifty-five percent with pathological drinking style, nineteen percent with problematic consumption, and seventeen percent with severe consequences.

How do the three components interrelate? In terms of correlations, the three components show rs between each

Table 8. Problem Drinking: Frequency of Problem Drinking Components by Sex for Q_2 Sample, Drinkers Only.

Q_1 percentages, measured somewhat differently than Q_2 percentages, are given in parentheses.

Drinking Style

	No Pathology	Moderate Pathology	Severe Pathology
Males	10(28)	35(47)	55(25)
Females	14(43)	31(39)	55(18)
Overall	12(34)	33(44)	55(22)

Consumption

	Light	Moderate	Problematic
Males	52(59)	26(13)	22(28)
Females	62(73)	23(9)	15(18)
Overall	57(65)	24(11)	19(24)

Consequences

	No Consequences	Medium Consequences	Severe Consequences
Males	60(62)	21(18)	19(20)
Females	67(70)	17(18)	16(12)
Overall	64(66)	19(18)	17(16)

other of from .42 to .50. However, a more complete breakdown revealed that one hundred percent of the severe consequences youth and ninety-two percent of the problematic consumption youth also had pathological drinking styles. However, over half of those youth who were problematic consumers were not in the severe consequences group. Hence knowing that a person is high in consequences or high in consumption predicts with near certainty a pathological drinking style, but knowing that he is high in consumption predicts with only fifty percent certainty that he has suffered severe consequences.

Table 9. Drinking Style and the Prediction of Problem Drinking. Items on Q_1 and Q_2 defining pathological drinking style. Percentages and correlations are given for **drinkers only**. Where both samples are given, Q_1 percentages and correlations are given in parentheses. All correlations are rounded down to the nearest tenth.

Drinking Style Items:	Percent of Drinkers	Prediction of Problem Drinking			
		Drinking Style	Consumption	Consequences	Overall Problems (Q_2 only)
Reasons for Drinking					
Makes popular (Q_1)	8	.2	.1	.1	.1
Get out of studying	2(4)	.1(.2)	.1(.1)	.1(.2)	.1
Worried about home	10(8)	.2(.4)	.1(.2)	.2(.3)	.2
At ease on date (Q_1)	13	.4	.3	.3	
Feel stronger (Q_1)	9	.4	.2	.3	
Do things better	7(6)	.2(.3)	.2(.1)	.2(.2)	.2
Feel more together (Q_2)	18	.3	.2	.2	.3
Feel more relaxed with opposite sex (Q_2)	23	.3	.3	.3	.3
People like me better (Q_2)	8	.1	.1	.2	.1
Helps to forget worries (Q_2)	22	.4	.3	.3	.3
Cheers me up when in a bad mood (Q_2)	29	.4	.3	.3	.4
Need it when tense and nervous (Q_2)	13	.2	.2	.2	.2

		Prediction of Problem Drinking			
Drinking Style Items:	Percent of Drinkers	Drinking Style	Consumption	Consequences	Overall Problems (Q2 only)
Change the way I feel (Q2)	29	.4	.4	.3	.4
*Feel better around people (Q2)	27	.3	.3	.3	.3
*To celebrate (Q2)	85	.3	.2	.1	.2
*No special reason (Q2)	52	.1	.1	.1	.1
Symptomatic Drinking					
Borrow or do without for drink	10(8)	.2(.5)	.2(.3)	.3(.4)	.4
Skip meals for drink (Q2)	17	.3	.3	.4	.4
Gulp drinks (Q2)	53	.5	.3	.3	.4
Drink before party (Q2)	40	.5	.4	.4	.4
Hands shake (Q2)	6	.3	.3	.4	.4
Morning drink (Q2)	15	.3	.3	.4	.4
Guilty or bummed out after drinking	21(17)	.3(.4)	.1(.1)	.3(.3)	.2
Memory lapse	37(28)	.5(.6)	.4(.4)	.4(.4)	.5
Binge Drinking					
Stayed high for whole day (Q2)	13	.3	.3	.4	.5
Stayed high for two or more days (Q2)	4	.1	.1	.2	.2

(Table 9, *continued*)

| | | Prediction of Problem Drinking | | | |
	Percent of Drinkers	Drinking Style	Consumption	Consequences	Overall Problems (Q2 only)
Drinking Style Items:					
Problematic Intake					
Prefers friends who drink	25(6)	.3(.2)	.4(.2)	.3(.1)	.3
Thinks has drinking problem	4(2)	.1(.2)	.1(.1)	.2(.2)	.2
Drinks alone	21(21)	.3(.4)	.2(.2)	.2(.2)	.2
Worries about his drinking (Q2)	7	.1	.1	.3	.2
Drinks more than friends (Q2)	13	.4	.2	.2	
*Drinks till nothing left	28(28)	.4(.6)	.5(.5)	.4(.4)	.5
Turns off to talks on drinking (Q1)	19	.3	.1	.1	
Belligerence					
Gets mad when drinking (Q2)	18	.3	.2	.4	.4
Gets into heated arguments (Q2)	10	.2	.2	.3	.3
Gets into fights (Q2)	9	.2	.2	.3	.3

*Not included in Problem Drinking measure of Drinking Style.

Table 10. Consumption: Frequency and Quantity of Drinking and Prediction of Problem Drinking.

Q_2 and Q_1 samples, **drinkers only.** When both samples are given, Q_1 percentages and correlations are given in parentheses. Correlations are rounded down to the nearest tenth.

Consumption Items:	Percent of Drinkers	Prediction of Problem Drinking			
		Drinking Style	Consumption	Consequences	Overall Problems (Q_2 only)
Frequency of Drinking Occasions		.5(.5)	.7	.4(.4)	.5
At least one time per year (Q_2)	94				
At least two or three times per year (Q_2)	87				
At least one time per month	61(47)				
At least two or three times per month (Q_2)	41				
At least one time per week	21(35)				
At least two or three times per week (Q_2)	10				
Every day	1.4(4)				

(Table 10, *continued*)

Consumption Items:	Percent of Drinkers	Prediction of Problem Drinking			
		Drinking Style	Consumption	Consequences	Overall Problems (Q2 only)
*Frequency of "Drunk" Occasions (Q2)		.6	.6	.4	.5
At least one time per year	50				
At least two or three times per year	40				
At least one time per month	25				
At least two or three times per month	13				
At least one time per week	6				
At least two or three times per week	2				
Every day	.4				
*Frequency of "High" Occasions (Q2)		.5	.4	.4	.5
At least once in a while	64				
At least more than half the time	31				
Nearly every time	17				
*Drinks more frequently than friends (Q2)	11	.1	.1	.2	.2
*Drinks more than friends (Q1)	13	.4	.2	.2	
Has had drink in last week (Q1)	48	.4	.6	.2	

| | | Prediction of Problem Drinking | | | |
Consumption Items:	Percent of Drinkers	Drinking Style	Consumption	Consequences	Overall Problems (Q2 only)
Quantity Items					
Number of drinks per occasion (Q2)		.4	.6	.3	.5
At least three	50				
At least five	24				
At least eight	5				
*Drinks more than two or three sometimes (Q2)	49	.5	.5	.3	.5
When drinks, has more than three (Q1)	34	.5	.7	.3	
*Usually ends up drinking more than friends (Q2)	13	.2	.2	.2	.2
*Sometimes drinks till nothing left to drink	28(28)	.4(.6)	.5(.5)	.4(.4)	.5

*Items not included in Problem Drinking measures of Consumption.

Table 11. Consequences of Drinking and Prediction of Problem Drinking. (Note: Q_1 and Q_2 samples, **drinkers only.** When both samples are given, Q_1 percentages and correlations are given in parentheses.)

Consequences Items:	Percent of Drinkers	Prediction of Problem Drinking			Overall Problems (Q_2 only)
		Drinking Style	Consumption	Consequences	
Home					
Got into trouble at home/ drinking (Q_1)	15	.4	.2	.6	
School					
Missed school/drinking	9(4)	.2(.2)	.2(.1)	.5(.3)	.5
Missed school/hangover (Q_2)	8	.2	.2	.4	.3
Missed class to have a drink (Q_2)	8	.2	.3	.5	.4
Social Effects					
Loss of friends/drinking	5(4)	.1(.2)	.1(.1)	.3(.4)	.3
Reputation hurt/drinking	7(16)	.2(.2)	.1(.1)	.4(.6)	.3
Trouble outside home/drinking	10(14)	.2(.4)	.2(.4)	.5(.7)	.4
Loss of job/drinking (Q_2)	0.7	—	—	.1	.1
Physical Effects					
Accident/drinking (Q_2)	6	.2	.2	.3	.3
Worries about health/ drinking (Q_2)	14	.2	.1	.5	.3
Hospitalized/drinking	1(2)	.1(.1)	.1(.1)	.1(.2)	.1
Police Problems					
Trouble with police/drinking	7(8)	.2(.3)	.1(.3)	.4(.6)	.4

172

Potential Problem Drinkers, Problem Drinkers, and Alcoholics by Grade. Given the three problem drinking components established above, we will define, for present purposes, the notions of "potential problem drinker," "problem drinker," and "alcoholic" according to the number of problem drinking components present in a given individual's profile.

Any individual who has scored problematic on at least one of the three components is designated a "potential problem drinker." Out of the pool of potential problem drinkers, those who are problematic on at least two components are designated "problem drinkers." Of the problem drinkers, those who are problematic on all three components are designated "alcoholics." Thus estimates of the number of alcoholics in our sample are conservative, inasmuch as a person must satisfy all three kinds of definitions of alcoholism to be designated an alcoholic.

As noted above, those who are problematic in consumption or in consequences are nearly certain to be problematic in drinking style. That is, those here designated as potential problem drinkers (fifty-six percent) are nearly certain to be those with a pathological drinking style (fifty-five percent). Therefore, we can redefine potential problem drinkers as those who have a pathological drinking style. Of these, those who are problem drinkers are also problematic in either consumption or consequences, and those who are alcoholics are also problematic in both consumption and consequences.

The individual problem drinking components and their combinations are shown in Table 12 for the various grade levels. First, considering overall incidence rates, by our definitions, fifty-six percent of the drinkers in our sample are at least potential problem drinkers, twenty-seven percent are at least problem drinkers, and eight percent are alcoholics.

Expressed in terms of the pool of potential problem drinkers, fourteen percent of potential problem drinkers are alcoholics, and thirty-four percent are problem drinkers but not alcoholics. Viewed as separate, rather than inclusive, categories, the proportion of nonabstainers who are alcoholics is eight percent, nineteen percent are problem drinkers but not alcoholics, and an additional twenty-nine percent are potential problem drinkers but not problem drinkers or alcoholics.

Table 12. Problem Drinking: Change in Problem Drinking Components Over Grade (percent).

Q₂ sample, **drinkers only,** N = 990. Percentages given are those in the most severe problem drinking category for one component (Potential Problem Drinkers), for at least two components (Problem Drinkers), and for all three components (Alcoholics).

| | Grade | | | | | |
	4-6 (N=172)	7-8 (N=219)	9-10 (N=235)	11-12 (N=273)	College (N=91)	Overall
Individual Components						
Pathological Style	23	47	56	73	76	**55**
Problematic Consumption	4	11	22	28	27	**19**
Severe Consequences	6	11	18	25	32	**17**
At Least One Component						
"Potential Problem Drinkers"	26	47	59	73	77	**56**
At Least Two Components						
"Problem Drinkers"	6	17	29	40	42	**27**
All Three Components						
"Alcoholics"	1.2	4	8	12	16	**8**

If we include the total sample (N=1,507)) of both drinkers and abstainers, then five percent are alcoholics, an additional twelve percent are problem drinkers (exclusively), and an additional nineteen percent are potential problem drinkers (exclusively). Therefore, out of the total sample, thirty-six percent of the youth population (mean age, 14.1) are at least potential problem drinkers.

Returning to Table 12, the problem drinking components are broken down for grade levels. Considering the problem drinking components, pathological drinking style occurs in about one-fourth of all elementary school drinkers, in about one-half of junior high and early high school students, and in about three-fourths of eleventh and twelfth graders and college students. Problematic consumption ranges from four percent in grades four to six to twenty-seven percent for college students. As was shown earlier for heavy drinking, the greatest increase in problematic consumption occurs between junior high and high school. Severe consequences of drinking increase uniformly from six percent for grades four to six to thirty-two percent for college students.

In regard to the category of potential problem drinkers, which has an almost perfect overlap with pathological style, the greatest jump is between elementary school and junior high school in the proportion of drinkers who are (at least) potential problem drinkers. Persons who are (at least) problem drinkers increase uniformly from six percent in grade school to forty percent at the end of high school. Alcoholics also increase uniformly, from 1.2 percent in grade school to sixteen percent in college.

If we assume that those who become problem drinkers and alcoholics in the later grades are recruited from the ranks of the potential problem drinkers of the earlier grades, then it is quite plausible that attempts to reduce the incidence of potential problem drinkers in the grade school and junior high school would eventually reduce the ranks of problem drinking and alcoholism in the later grades. This possibility, supported by the nearly perfect overlap between pathological style and the other two components, could well take the form of an hypothesis for a prevention-oriented program.

Overall Problems Typology. Cahalan and Room, in *Problem Drinking among American Men*, formed a partitioning of their 1969 national survey data to reflect a current problems score, on the basis of which estimates of alcoholism in the male population are often made. We constructed an overall problems score to correspond as closely as possible to the current problem score of Cahalan and Room (defined precisely in Appendix C).

The overall problems typology, defined for drinkers only, consists of 1) no problems (twelve percent of the Q_2 drinkers), 2) problems of at least minimal severity but not 3) and 4) (fifty-seven percent), 3) heavy or binge drinking but not 4) (fourteen percent), and 4) severe consequences (seventeen percent). The typology is broken down by sex in Table 13. Table 13 also compares our overall problems typology for males with the parallel Cahalan and Room typology for male adults twenty-one years and over in 1969.

Table 13. Overall Problem Percentages for Males and Females in the Q_2 Sample. Comparable percentages for **male adults** from Cahalan & Room are given in parentheses. **Drinkers only.**

	Overall Problems			
	No Problems	Minimal Severity	Heavy Drinking or Binge Drinking	Severe Consequences
Females	14	58	12	16
Males	10 (45)	56 (25)	15 (14)	19 (16)
Overall	12	57	14	17

While sixteen percent of the adult male drinkers in the 1969 national survey were classified in the most severe category, nineteen percent of the current youth sample (Q_2) were so classified. The rates for heavy or binge drinking (but not severe consequences) are about the same for both the youth and adult samples.

The primary difference between the two male samples occurs in the no problem and minimal severity categories. *Young males are much more likely than adult males to have problems of at least minimal severity if they drink.*

Finally, estimating from the overall problems typology, the rate of problem drinking or alcoholism among all drinking youth in our sample, both male and female, is seventeen percent. If abstainers are included, the overall rate is eleven percent in the total youth sample.

Frequency of "Drunk" Occasions. Table 10 shows the frequency of self-reported "drunk" occasions for drinkers, along with the frequency of drinking occasions for drinkers. Considering all drinkers, fifty percent report getting drunk at least once per year, twenty-five percent at least once a month, and six percent at least once per week.

Taking drinking frequency into consideration, of those who drink at least once per year, over fifty percent get drunk at least once per year; of those who drink at least once per month, forty percent get drunk at least once per month; of those who drink at least once a week, thirty percent get drunk at least once a week; and of those who drink daily, thirty percent get drunk daily. Thus as drinking frequency increases, reported drunkenness uniformly decreases and eventually levels off at about twenty to thirty percent.

Social/Attitudinal Predictors of Problem Drinking. The last four columns of Tables 6 and 7 give the correlation coefficients (rounded down to the lowest tenth) between social/attitudinal variables and problem drinking among nonabstainers. The measures of problem drinking employed were the three problem drinking components—drinking style, consumption, and consequences, together with the overall problems typology, discussed earlier, which combines aspects of all three components, but which is weighted most heavily by consequences.

As was the case with drinker status, the strongest predictors among the social differentiations (Table 6) were age and grade. Sex was a low and inconsistent predictor of problem drinking for the Q_1 and Q_2 samples. For the Q_2 sample, only consumption was significantly affected by sex, with males yielding a higher incidence of heavy consumption than females. Family drinker status did not predict problem drinking, unless there was a drinking problem in the family. If the father is dead, if family size is large, and if the youth does not live with both parents, problem drinking is slightly, but significantly, higher. Independence items are also small but reliable predictors of problem drinking.

Socioeconomic status was completely unrelated to problem drinking incidence. Church attendance was a low but reliable predictor (negatively) of problem drinking.

Turning to Table 7, as was the case for the prediction of drinker status, peer group, drug use, and police trouble variables were strong predictors of problem drinking ($rs > .3$). The only other strong predictors ($rs > .3$) were self-ascribed drinker status (says he or she is a "person who drinks"), and the belief that sex and drinking go together. It is noteworthy that these latter two attitudinal variables are better predictors of problem drinking than of drinker status (Column 2).

All the school variables were weak, but reliable, predictors of problem drinking. Although the self-concept variables were generally nonpredictive of drinker status, whether they see themselves as happy persons, feel different, feel depressed, or like themselves did significantly, if weakly, predict at least one of the problem drinking criteria.

Summary of the problem drinking results. Three components of problem drinking were defined for drinkers and combined to define "potential problem drinking" (twenty-nine percent), "problem drinking" (nineteen percent), and "alcoholism" (eight percent) for present purposes. Fifty-six percent of the sample were at least potential problem drinkers. The overall problems typology placed the alcoholism rate at eleven percent for the total youth sample, including abstainers. Over one-half of all nonabstainers report getting drunk at least once a year, and one fourth report getting drunk at least once a month. The strongest social/attitudinal determinants of problem drinking were age, grade, peer group drinking, drug use, self-ascribed drinker status, police trouble, and belief that sex and drinking go together.

C. Drinking-Related Predictors of Problem Drinking

Tables 9, 10, and 11 show the drinking items relating to the three problem drinking components—style, consumption, and consequences. In the present discussion, we will highlight those items that predicted the summary measure of overall problems (in the righthand column of each table) with correlation coefficients greater than .4.

Pathological Drinking Style. The righthand column of Table 9 displays the rs (rounded down to the lowest tenth) between the drinking style item and the overall problems measure. Among reasons for drinking, "cheers me up when in a bad mood" and "to change the way I feel" are the best discriminating items for problem drinking.

Seven out of eight of the symptomatic drinking items discriminated problem drinkers with $r > .4$. This is clearly the best set of predictors among the style items. Included here are the central nervous system effects of heavy drinking, such as shakes and memory lapse. Turning to column 1, it is interesting to note the high proportions of drinkers who show symptomatic drinking signs.

The remaining three items that strongly discriminate problem drinking are binge drinking, "drinks till nothing left," and "gets mad when drinks."

Problematic Consumption. Among items assessing frequency of consumption (Table 10), the best predictors of overall problems were frequency of drinking occasions, frequency of "drunk" occasions, and frequency of occasions getting "high." Among the quantity items, the best predictors were "number of drinks per occasion," "drinks more than two or three," and "drinks till nothing left."

It is instructive to note the incidence rates on the "number of drinks per occasion" item (column 1). Fifty percent of all drinkers have at least three drinks per occasion, and twenty-five percent have at least five per occasion, and five have at least eight drinks.

Severe Consequences. Of the consequences items (Table 11), the best discriminating items ($rs > .4$) are "missed school due to drinking," "missed class to have a drink" "trouble outside home due to drinking," and "trouble with police due to drinking." Also a strong predictor from the Pilot Questionnaire was the item, "got into trouble at home due to drinking." Nearly all the rest of the items are also strong predictors, with $rs > .3$. Note that the highest single incidence rate (column 1) is the home trouble item (fifteen percent).

These best-discriminating items for problem drinking will be employed in the design of the diagnostic instrument to be constructed in the following section.

D. Youth Diagnostic Screening Tests for Preteens and Teenagers

Previous brief screening instruments such as the Twenty Questions about Alcohol for Youth (1) have not been based on correlations with problem drinking, but rather have been chosen on the basis of *a priori* face validity. The screening tests presented in this section are based on items which have significant relationships to our indices of problem drinking.

The first screening test was designed to screen preteen non-drinkers for those who are at risk of developing a drinking problem if and when they begin to drink. The second screening test is designed to tap potential problem drinkers, problem drinkers, and alcoholics among teenagers who drink, and to assess the severity problem with each of the problem drinking components—style, consumption, and consequences.

At-Risk Screening Test for Nondrinking Preteens

The At-Risk Screening Test is based on the nondrinking-related items from the two youth surveys (see Tables 6 and 7). Those items were selected from Tables 6 and 7 *which correlated significantly with at least two of the problem drinking indices.* If the item was present on both the Q_1 and Q_2 surveys, then the item selected had to correlate significantly with at least two problem drinking indices for both the main sample (Q_2) and the replication sample (Q_1).

The resultant screening test for at-risk youth is given in Table 14. Item 26 "Would you sometimes like to be a person who drinks?" was modified from the highly predictive Q_2 item "Do you consider yourself as a person who drinks?" The rest of the items are exactly as presented in the surveys (Appendices A and B).

The At-Risk Test is intended for preteens, most of whom are not yet drinkers. Item 27 determines whether or not the respondent is of drinker status. This item is weighted double the weight of the other items, because *if the preteenager already drinks at this age, he is probably already at-risk for problem drinking.* As Jessor and Jessor (3) have demonstrated, the earlier the age of onset of drinker status, the greater the likelihood of developing a drinking problem by high school age.

Unless otherwise indicated alongside the item, all items are to be given a score of 1 for a "Yes" response. The items weighted double (given a score of 2) were not only significantly related to problem drinking, but also met the further criterion of correlating greater than .2 with the overall problems index.

The At-Risk Screening Test results in at-risk scores from 0 to 35. As recommended in Part E of this report, those elementary school and junior high school children who score in the upper percentiles of this test are prime candidates for problem drinking prevention strategies.

Table 14. Youth Diagnostic Screening Test
(Part I: At Risk for Problem Drinking)

Part I of the Test consists of nondrinking items and can be used for young nondrinkers as a selection device for prevention strategies. Items were selected from Q_1 and Q_2 surveys which correlated significantly with at least two of the Problem Drinking indices on *both* surveys (when available). (All items are scored 1 for a "Yes" response unless otherwise indicated. Total score can range from 0 to 35.)

1. Are you male or female? (No score.)
2. How old are you? (No score.)
3. Have you ever lived with anyone other than your parents?
4. Do you usually have a job outside your home?
5. Do you go to church or another established religious institution? (Score 1 for "No" response.)
6. Do you feel that you're on your own?
7. Does anyone in your family have a problem with drinking?
8. Did you have your first drink at home? (Score 1 for "No.")
9. Do you sometimes turn off to people who give talks on alcoholism or drinking?
10. Do you believe drinking makes people more popular?
11. Have you ever gotten into trouble at school?
12. Do you get into trouble at school often?
13. Do you like school most of the time? (Score 1 for "No" response.)

14. Do you generally get good grades in school? (Score 1 for "No" response.)
15. Do you often have times when you're depressed or really down?
16. Would you say that you are a happy person? (Score 1 for "No" response.)
17. Have you ever heard of Alateen?
18. Do you sometimes hang out with kids who drink? (Score 2 for "Yes" response.)
19. Do you prefer to be with friends who drink? (Score 2 for "Yes" response.)
20. Do you and your friends think sex and drinking go together? (Score 2 for "Yes" response)
21. Do you use or have you ever used drugs? (Score 2 for "Yes" response.)
22. Do you favor pot over alcohol? (Score 2 for "Yes" response.)
23. Do you smoke cigarettes regularly? (Score 2 for "Yes" response.)
24. Have you ever been busted for possession of an illegal drug? (Score 2 for "Yes" response.)
25. Have you ever gotten into trouble with the police? (Score 2 for "Yes" response.)
26. Would you sometimes like to be a person who drinks? (Score 2 for "Yes" response.)
27. Have you ever had a drink of beer, wine, or liquor *more than two or three times in your life?* (Score 2 for "Yes" response.)

Problem Drinking Screening Test for Teenagers

The Problem Drinking Screening Test, designed for those youth who are already of drinker status, is based on both drinking and nondrinking-related items from the Q_1 and Q_2 surveys (Tables 6, 7, 9, 10, 11). Those items were selected which showed a correlation of greater than .3 with one of the three problem drinking component indices, other than the component index which included them as problem drinking items. (In other words, a pathological style item, such as "drinks alone," must correlate over .3 with either the consumption component or the consequences component in order to be included in the Problem Drinking Screening Test.) In addition, items from the Q_2 survey had to meet the further criterion of correlating over .3 with the overall problems summary index.

Table 15 presents the Problem Drinking Screening Test. All items are scored 1 for a "Yes" response unless otherwise indicated. Items weighted double (scored 2) met rigorous criterion of correlating over .5 with the overall problems summary index (as seen in Tables 9-11). The screening test ranges in score from 0 to 44, higher numbers associated with severity of problem drinking.

From Table 15, items 3 through 8 are those that meet the criteria from the nondrinking-related questions. Items 9-28 and 39-40 measure the drinking style component of problem drinking; items 29-34 measure the consumption component; items 35-38 measure the consequences component.

The style component is broken into subcomponents as follows: Items 9 and 10 are the peer group items, items 11-17 are the reasons for drinking items, items 18-28 are symptomatic drinking items (including binge drinking and belligerence), and items 39-40 are the control items.

1. Determination of Type and Severity of Problem Drinking. A young person who scores at least 3 on the nondrinking items (items 3-8), *and* at least 5 on the pathological style items (items 9-28 and 39-40), *and* at least 4 on the problematic consumption items (items 29-34), *and* at least 2 on the consequences items (items 35-38) is diagnosed an "alcoholic," on the basis of our earlier definition. This diagnosis corresponds to our criterion that an alcoholic is problematic on all three of the problem drinking components.

2. Determination of Problem Drinking. A person who scores at least 3 on the nondrinking items, and scores the same as that required for an alcoholic diagnosis on two of the three problem drinking components, is diagnosed a "problem drinker," but not an alcoholic. This diagnosis corresponds to our earlier criterion that a problem drinker must be problematic on more than one of the problem drinking components.

3. Determination of Potential Problem Drinking. A person who scores at least 3 on the nondrinking items, and scores the same as that required for an alcoholic diagnosis on one of the three problem drinking components is diagnosed a "potential problem drinker." This diagnosis corresponds to our earlier criterion that a potential problem drinker must be problematic on one of the components.

Preliminary Validation of the Problem Drinking Screening Test. As mentioned in Part A, twelve young people were included in the Q_1 sample who were currently being treated at the ACOC youth program. These youth were referred by the probation department as having severe drinking problems. It is this kind of youth that we have in mind when the diagnosis of teenage alcoholism is made.

Eleven of the twelve were male, and the mean age of the subsample was eighteen. We have data from these problem youth on eighteen items of the Problem Drinking Screening Test. Scores on these items were extrapolated to estimate their average scores on the test components.

The "alcoholic" youth scored an average of 4.5 on the nondrinking component, 15.0 on the pathological style component, 6.2 on the consumption component, and 3.2 on the consequences component. When we compare these mean scores for the twelve "alcoholic" youth to the cutoff scores established above for the alcoholism diagnosis, it is seen that the "average" alcoholic youth was correctly classified as an alcoholic, inasmuch as he is beyond the cutoff point on all three problem drinking components as well as on the nondrinking component.

We stress that these cutoff points at this point are tentative and subject to further validation for our three problem drinking categories. It is of interest to note that the mean total score on the Problem Drinking Screening Test for the "alcoholic" youth was 29, out of a possible 44. Continued testing of problem drinking and alcoholic youth will develop normative cutoff points for the total score.

The Problem Drinking Screening Test, then, can produce a total score to diagnose the severity of problem drinking, and can, for each person, classify his dominant type of drinking problem according to his three component scores on the pathological style, consumption, and consequences dimensions.

Table 15. Youth Diagnostic Screening Test (Part II: Problem Drinking).

Items were selected from the Q_1 and Q_2 Surveys that correlated greater than .3 both with independent indices of Problem Drinking *and* with the Overall Problems index (for Q_2 items). (All items are scored 1 for a "Yes" response unless otherwise indicated. Total Score can range from 0 to 44.)

1. Are you male or female? (No score.)
2. How old are you? (No score.)
3. Do you use or have you ever used drugs?
4. Have you ever been busted for possession of an illegal drug?
5. Have you had a drink of beer, wine, or liquor *more than two or three times in your life?*
6. Do you consider yourself as a person who drinks?
7. Do you favor pot over alcohol?
8. Do you and your friends think sex and drinking go together?
9. Do you sometimes hang out with kids who drink?
10. Do you prefer to be with friends who drink?
11. Do you sometimes drink because it makes you feel more at ease on a date?

12. Do you sometimes drink because it makes you feel more relaxed with the opposite sex?

13. Do you sometimes drink because it makes you feel better around people?

14. Do you sometimes drink because it helps you forget your worries?

15. Do you sometimes drink because it helps to cheer you up when you're in a bad mood?

16. Do you sometimes drink to change the way you feel?

17. Do you sometimes drink because it makes you feel stronger?

18. Have you ever borrowed money or done without other things to buy alcohol?

19. Have you ever skipped meals while drinking?

20. Do you sometimes gulp down a drink rather than drink it slowly?

21. Do you sometimes drink before going to a party?

22. Do you ever notice that your hands shake when you wake up in the morning?

23. Have you ever taken a drink in the morning?

24. Have you ever felt guilty or bummed out after drinking?

25. Do you ever have times when you cannot remember some of what happened while drinking (Score 2 for "Yes" response.)

26. Have you ever stayed high drinking for a whole day? (Score 2 for "Yes" response.)

27. Do you ever get mad or get into a heated argument when you drink?

28. Have you ever gotten into a fight when drinking?

29. Do you sometimes drink until there's nothing left to drink? (Score 2 for "Yes" response.)

30. Would you say that you get "high" when you drink more than half the time? (Score 2 for "Yes" response.)

31. Would you say that you get "drunk" or "bombed" at least once a month or more? (Score 2 for "Yes" response.)

32. Have you had anything to drink in the last week?
33. When you drink, do you usually end up having more than four of whatever you're drinking? (Score 2 for "Yes" response.)
34. Would you say that you have a drink of beer, wine, or liquor at least once a week or more? (Score 2 for "Yes" response.)
35. Have you ever missed school or missed a class because of drinking? (Score 2 for "Yes" response.)
36. Have you ever gotten into trouble at home because of your drinking?
37. Have you ever gotten into trouble outside your home because of your drinking?
38. Have you ever gotten into trouble with the police because of drinking?
39. Do you sometimes get drunk when you didn't start out to get drunk?
40. Do you sometimes try to cut down on your drinking?

E. A Recommended Program for Prevention and Intervention

On the basis of the present findings on problem drinking rates among Orange County youth, the urgency of interception programs at all levels of youth hardly needs justification. The incidence of heavy drinking and problem drinking among youth is already higher than the most recent estimates for adults (Tables 5 and 13). The rate of problem drinking among those who drink jumps rapidly from six percent in grades four to six to seventeen percent in junior high school, leveling off at about forty percent in late high school (Table 12).

Our data strongly indicate that these problem drinkers become steadily recruited from a relatively large pool of potential or incipient problem drinkers who are already having problems of minimal severity (Table 12). Moreover, this pool is growing at an alarming rate, and our data indicate it is already twice as large as the adult pool of potential problem drinkers (Table 13).

The existing literature indicates that traditional alcoholism education programs have not been effective with our youth and that there are not many programs serving young alcohol offenders that have been demonstrated to work.*

Our data make clear that the target of prevention efforts must be the probable (at-risk) problem drinker and the potential problem drinker, both of whom can be diagnosed via the screening tests developed in Section D. At the present time, the most efficient targets of intervention (or treatment) efforts, in terms of ultimate benefit to society, are problem drinking youth who are recent entries into the juvenile justice system.

At the same time, the present data suggest a common strategy for prevention and intervention. It was noted in the text that the most powerful social predictors of problem drinking were the items relating to peer group behavior (Tables 6 and 7). These results indicate that a peer modeling approach to both prevention (at the preteen level) and treatment is apt to be most fruitful.

On the basis of the findings of this report, the Alcoholism Council of Orange County recommends a joint prevention/intervention program that would assume form as follows:

1. **General Statement of Purpose.** The purpose of the recommended program is to introduce and test a method for both the *prevention* of problem drinking in preteen youth and the *treatment* of teenage alcohol offenders. The program will be subjected to continuous ongoing evaluation to establish what procedures are most effective for what kinds of youth.

---

*Editor's note: There is an apparent gap between existing successful youth alcoholism programs and printed information about them. Only a few programs have been operating long enough to gauge their success in terms of recovery. So far, those programs with a high recovery rate seem to be known only in their own areas of the country.

2. Identification of Types of Problem Drinkers and At-Risk Preteens. Based on the present survey of youth alcohol patterns, instruments were proposed that are capable of 1) diagnosing kinds of problem drinking in youthful alcohol offenders referred by the juvenile justice system, and 2) identifying preteens *at risk* of developing into problem drinkers. These instruments must be further developed, by means of normative data, to enhance their validity and usefulness.

3. Peer Modeling Approach. The overall philosophy of the recommended approach is that intervention in youth must be accomplished by peer models at the level of both *attitudes* toward drinking and drinking *behavior.* Our research indicates that the behavior of peer reference groups is a strong predictor of problem drinking. Therefore, our attack on attitudes and behavior will utilize predominately the peer modeling approach. In addition, it is advisable to test the additional effectiveness of parent and family workshops among youthful offenders in our overall design.

a. Peer Counselors. It is recommended that a training program be initiated to provide peer counselors. These paraprofessional counselors will be selected from among young people who are both similar to their target groups on critical dimensions and who are screened for counseling aptitude.

b. Preteen Target Groups. Peer counselors will be selected and assigned to a number of elementary and junior high schools in Orange County. Awareness classes will be established at these schools, in cooperation with school counselors, for those identified as at-risk on the Preteen Diagnostic Test. Classes will be run weekly at each school.

c. Teenage Problem Drinkers. Youthful offenders referred by probation will be diagnosed as to type and severity of drinking problem and will be assigned to youth groups conducted by peer counselors. It is advisable, if possible, that offenders be assigned to youth groups in facilities in the community where they live. Depending on their diagnostic category, offenders will also be assigned to family workshops, to Alateen, or to young people's AA groups in their community. The assignment will be made in such a way as to systematically evaluate the impact each treatment makes.

d. Transition from Preteens to Teens. At-risk preteens subjected to awareness groups in primary and junior high schools will be systematically followed up when they reach secondary school, and will be carefully compared to at-risk preteens not exposed to awareness groups.

4. Specific Objectives of the Recommended Program.

a. To further develop reliable and valid screening instruments for at-risk preteenagers and for youthful offenders with alcohol problems.

b. To develop a training program for peer counselors, which will incorporate skills for both attitude change and behavioral change.

c. To provide continuous ongoing evaluation of the effectiveness of the peer modeling approach, in order to determine which subgroups of at-risk preteens and youthful offenders accrue benefits.

d. To assess the effectiveness of parent workshops and family therapy on outcome measures for the youth offenders.

e. To assess for youth offenders the effectiveness of attendance at Alateen and young people's AA groups.

5. Peer Model Training Program.
Young people will be carefully selected and taught skills in reconstructive, reeducative, and supportive therapy. Each peer counselor will be under constant supervision and will provide for his group a packet of self-help materials for specific goal attainment and for attitude change among group members.

6. Program Evaluation. It is recommended that the program be placed within an action-research framework. That is, the program at all levels will be subject to continuous ongoing evaluation, so that feedback about effective methods will cause them to be immediately instituted, and feedback about ineffective methods will cause them to be immediately discarded.

a. Preteens. Base-line measurements will be taken at all elementary and junior high schools on 1) types and frequency of reported alcohol-related school problems, and 2) the proportion of the school populations who are at-risk or potential problem drinkers. At six-month intervals, measures will again be taken of alcohol-related school problems at *both* schools where the peer modeling approach is instituted and at schools *not* selected for the program. Moreover, peer and teacher ratings of at-risk students will also be taken at these intervals. For transition measurements, at-risk students exposed to our program will be carefully measured when they reach high school, and will be compared to similar students *not* exposed to the program.

b. Teen Problem Drinkers. Teen problem drinkers referred to our program will be compared at six-month intervals with teen problem drinkers not referred to our program in terms of a variety of outcome measures, including recidivism, drinking behavior, vocational health, interpersonal health, and emotional health. Furthermore, it will be determined which kinds of offenders benefit from the youth groups, family therapy, and parent workshops.

7. Significance of the Recommended Program. The recommended program for Orange County youth is designed primarily to assess the peer modeling approach to potential problem drinkers and to teenage alcohol offenders. The program design is equipped to zero in on what types of preteens and teens benefit from this approach, and which types are left unaffected by it both in the short run, and, in the case of preteens, in the long run (when they reach high school). The information obtained from such a program with a built-in continuous feedback system and appropriate controls can be easily generalized to and implemented by other agencies concerned with the early identification and treatment of teenage drinking problems.

References

1. "Twenty Questions about Alcohol for Youth." Alcoholism Council of Orange County, Santa Ana, Calif.

2. Maddox, G. L., and McCall, B. C. *Drinking among Teen-Agers.* New Brunswick, N.J.: Rutgers Center of Alcohol Studies, 1964.

3. Jessor, R., and Jessor, S. L. "Adolescent Development and the Onset of Drinking." *Journal of Studies on Alcohol, 36,* 27-55, 1975.

4. Cahalan, D., and Room, R. *Problem Drinking among American Men.* New Brunswick, N.J.: Rutgers Center of Alcohol Studies, 1974.

5. Cahalan, D., Cisin, I., and Crossley, H. *American Drinking Practices.* New Brunswick, N.J.: Rutgers Center of Alcohol Studies, 1969.

6. Pernanen, K. "Validity of Survey Data on Alcohol Use." Y. Israel (Ed.), *Research Advances in Alcohol and Drug Problems,* Vol. 1, New York: John Wiley & Sons, Inc., 1974.

7. Bacon, S. Reports of Meetings: Defining Adolescent Alcohol Use. *Journal of Studies on Alcohol, 38,* 1976.

8. Armor, D. J., Polich, M. M., and Stambul, H. B. *Alcoholism and Treatment.* Santa Monica, Calif. Rand Corporation, 1976.

Appendix A:
The Pilot Questionnaire (Q$_1$)

Pilot Questionnaire

1. How old are you?
2. What grade are you in?
3. Are you a boy or a girl?
4. How many older brothers and sisters do you have?
5. How many younger brothers and sisters do you have?
6. Is your mother living?
7. Is your father living?
8. Are your parents living together?
9. Have you ever lived with anyone other than your parents?
10. What kind of work does your father do?
11. Does your mother work?
12. Do you go to church?
13. Do you go to church every week or most every week?
14. Do you ever work outside your home for extra money?
15. Does your mother or father drink every day or almost every day?
16. Does your mother ever drink?
17. Does your father ever drink?
18. Have you ever tasted alcohol?
19. Have you had anything to drink in the last week?
20. How often do you drink alcohol?
    a. Never.
    b. Hardly ever
    c. Holidays (Christmas, New Year's, etc.)
    d. Once a year
    e. Twice a year
    f. Once a month
    g. Once a week
    h. On weekends
    i. After school or work
21. Do you ever miss school because of drinking?
22. Do you sometimes drink to feel better?
23. Do you sometimes drink because it makes you think you can do things better?

24. Do you sometimes drink because it makes you feel better around people?
25. Do you ever drink alone?
26. Does drinking make you more popular with your friends?
27. Does drinking ever hurt your reputation?
28. Do you ever drink to get out of studying?
29. Do you ever drink because you're worried about what's going on at home?
30. Do you ever feel guilty or bummed out after drinking?
31. Does it ever bother you if someone says you drink too much?
32. Do you feel more at ease on a date when drinking?
33. Do you feel more at ease with people when drinking?
34. Have you ever gotten into trouble at home because of your drinking?
35. Have you ever gotten into trouble outside your home because of your drinking?
36. Do you ever borrow money or "do without" other things to be able to buy something to drink?
37. Have you ever gotten into trouble with the police because of your drinking?
38. Do you ever feel stronger when you drink?
39. Have you ever lost friends due to your drinking?
40. Do you drink more than your friends?
41. Do you sometimes hang out with kids who drink?
42. Do you sometimes drink until there's nothing left to drink?
43. Do you ever wake up and can't remember some of what happened the night before?
44. Have you ever been to a hospital for drinking?
45. Do you sometimes turn off to people who talk about alcoholics or drinking among kids?
46. Do you *think* you have a problem with drinking?
47. Does anyone in your family have a problem with drinking?

48. Have you ever heard of Alateen?
49. Do you ever use any drugs besides alcohol?
50. Have you ever been busted for possession of an illegal drug?
51. Do you favor pot over alcohol?
52. Did you have your first drink at home?
53. When you drink, do you have more than three of whatever you're drinking?
54. Do you and your friends think sex and drinking go together?
55. What kind of work does your mother do?
56. Do you prefer to associate with friends who drink?
57. Do you live with both of your parents?
58. Do you feel more at ease with the opposite sex when drinking?

Appendix B:
The Youth Drinking
Questionnaire (Q$_2$)

Alcoholism Council of Orange County Youth Drinking Questionnaire, 1976

This questionnaire will be administered orally in the classroom by a trained interviewer associated with the Alcoholism Council of Orange County. The questions to be read consist of those on the attached pages. Response sheets will be distributed to each of the students in the classes. Students will indicate their responses to each question read on this response sheet. After the questionnaires are completed, they will hand them to the interviewer with no names on the sheet. That is, the questionnaires will be filled out completely anonymously.

Instructions:

Do *not* put your name on the response sheet. This is a completely anonymous questionnaire—no one will know about your answers except you, because there will be no names on the sheet. The purpose of this questionnaire is to find out the drinking patterns of young people.

I will read several questions about drinking alcoholic beverages. Simply indicate your response on the response sheet in front of you for the appropriate question number. Remember we are talking about drinking drinks that contain *alcohol*, such as beer, wine, ales, and hard liquors such as whiskey, vodka, brandy and after-dinner liqueurs. Try to answer the questions as honestly and clearly as you can. Most of the questions are answered Yes or No. If Yes, put a check *in front of* the Yes on your response sheet. If No, put a check *in front of* the No on your response sheet. Sometimes you will find it hard to decide between Yes and No, but *do not* leave it blank. If you cannot make up your mind, select the answer that comes *closest* to what you think.

The questions about drinking always refer to your *whole life*—so that if a question is like "Do you ever drink?", remember that this means "Have you ever had something to drink *sometime in your life?*"

Please let us have *no talking* of any kind while filling out the response sheet. Concentrate on your own answers and don't look around at your neighbor's answers. If I go too fast for you, raise your hand and I will repeat the question and slow down. Do not shout out to me—just raise your hand.

Remember, do *not* put your name on the response sheet. No one will know what answers you put down except you. O.K., are we ready to begin?

(INTERVIEWER: AFTER FINISHING THE QUESTIONNAIRE, ASK THE CLASS TO GO BACK OVER THEIR RESPONSE SHEETS AND LOOK FOR ANSWERS LEFT BLANK. REPEAT THE QUESTIONS SO THAT STUDENTS HAVE NO BLANKS ON THEIR SHEETS.)

1. How old are you?
2. What grade are you in?
3. Are you a male or a female?
4. How many older brothers and sisters do you have?
5. How many younger brothers and sisters do you have?
6. How many adults do you live with as part of your family (other than roomers or brothers and sisters)?
7. Is your father living?
8. What kind of work does your father (or stepfather) usually do?
9. Is your father (or stepfather) currently working?
10. Is your mother living?
11. What kind of work does your mother (or stepmother) usually do?
12. Are your parents living together?
13. Have you ever lived outside your home other than for just visiting?
14. Do you usually have a job outside your home?
15. Do you sometimes turn off to people who give talks on alcoholism or drinking?

16. Do you favor pot over alcohol?
17. Do you believe drinking makes people more popular?
18. Have you ever gotten into trouble at school?
19. Do you get into trouble at school often?
20. Have you ever gotten into trouble with the police?
21. Do you like school most of the time?
22. Do you often have times when you're depressed or really down?
23. Do you like yourself most of the time?
24. Would you say that you are a happy person?
25. Do you feel as if you are different from most people?
26. Do you generally get good grades in school?
27. Do you feel that you're on your own?
28. Have you ever heard of Alateen?
29. Have you ever gone to a meeting of Alcoholics Anonymous?
30. Do you use or have you ever used drugs?
31. Do you prefer to be with friends who drink?
32. Do you sometimes feel uncomfortable around members of the opposite sex?
33. Have you ever been busted for possession of an illegal drug?
34. Do you smoke cigarettes regularly?
35. Do you consider yourself as a person who drinks?
36. Have you ever had a drink of beer, wine, or liquor — not just a sip or a taste?
37. Have you had a drink of beer, wine, or liquor *more than two or three times in your life?*

IF YOU ANSWERED NO TO THE LAST QUESTION — THAT IS, IF YOU HAVE NOT HAD A DRINK MORE THAN TWO OR THREE TIMES IN YOUR LIFE — THEN MOST OF YOUR ANSWERS ON THE REST OF THE QUESTIONNAIRE WILL PROBABLY BE NO. EVEN IF THEY ARE NO, CONTINUE TO FILL OUT THE ANSWER SHEET ANYWAY.

38. People drink wine, beer, or liquor for different reasons. I will read some of the reasons people give for drinking. Answer Yes or No if sometimes you drink for that reason.
    a. I sometimes drink because it makes me feel more together.
    b. I sometimes drink because it makes me feel more relaxed with the opposite sex.
    c. I sometimes drink because it makes me feel better around people.
    d. I sometimes drink because it makes me do things better.
    e. I sometimes drink to get out of studying.
    f. I sometimes drink because other people seem to like me better when I drink.
    g. I sometimes drink because I am worried about what's going on at home.
    h. I sometimes drink because it helps me to forget my worries.
    i. I sometimes drink because it helps to cheer me up when I'm in a bad mood.
    j. I sometimes drink because I need it when I'm tense and nervous.
    k. I sometimes drink to change the way I feel.
    l. I sometimes drink to celebrate.
    m. Most of the time I don't drink for any special reason.
39. About how often do you have a drink of beer, wine, or liquor? Circle one on your answer sheet. (Circle a for "Less than once a year"; circle b . . .)
    a. Less than once a year
    b. About once a year
    c. About two or three times a year
    d. About once a month
    e. About two or three times a month
    f. About once a week
    g. About two or three times a week
    h. Every day or almost every day

40. Do you drink more frequently than your friends?
41. How often do you get high when you drink? Circle one on your answer sheet. (Circle a for "Nearly every time"; circle b . . .)
    a. Nearly every time
    b. More than half the time
    c. Less than half the time
    d. Once in a while
    e. Never
42. About how often do you get "drunk" or "bombed" when you drink? Circle one on your answer sheet. (Circle a for "Never"; circle b . . .)
    a. Never
    b. Less than once a year
    c. About once a year
    d. About two or three times a year
    e. About once a month
    f. About two or three times a month
    g. About once a week
    h. About two or three times a week
    i. Every day or almost every day
43. Do you ever drink more than two or three of whatever you're drinking?
44. When you drink, about how many drinks do you usually end up having? Write down one number.
45. When you drink, do you usually end up drinking more than your friends?
46. Do you sometimes drink until there's nothing left to drink?
47. Do you sometimes feel that you wish you could have a drink even though you can't have one?
48. Do you sometimes take a drink when you don't really want one?
49. Do you sometimes get drunk even when you didn't start out to get drunk?
50. Do you sometimes try to cut down on your drinking?

51. Does it ever bother you if someone says you drink too much?
52. Do you sometimes think you have a problem with drinking?
53. Do you ever drink alone?
54. Have you ever borrowed money or done without other things to buy alcohol?
55. Have you ever skipped meals while drinking?
56. Do you sometimes gulp down a drink rather than drink it slowly?
57. Do you sometimes drink before going to a party?
58. Do you ever get high drinking alone?
59. Do you ever notice that your hands shake when you wake up in the morning?
60. Have you ever taken a drink in the morning?
61. Have you ever stayed high drinking for a whole day?
62. Have you ever stayed high drinking for two or more days at a time?
63. Do you ever worry about your drinking?
64. Do you ever get mad at anyone when you drink?
65. Do you ever get into a heated argument when you drink?
66. Have you ever gotten into a fight when drinking?
67. Did you ever lose a friend or almost lose a friend because of your drinking?
68. Did you ever lose a job or nearly lose a job because of drinking?
69. Have you ever missed class to have a drink?
70. Have you ever missed school because of drinking?
71. Have you ever stayed away from school because of a bad hangover?
72. Have you ever gotten into trouble with the police because of drinking?
73. Have you ever been in an accident while drinking?
74. Do you ever worry about your health because of drinking?
75. Have you ever been to a hospital because of drinking?

76. Has drinking ever hurt your reputation?
77. Have you ever felt guilty or bummed out after drinking?
78. Do you ever have times when you cannot remember some of what happened while drinking?
79. Have you ever gotten into trouble outside your home because of your drinking?
80. Do you remember clearly the first time you had a drink?

Response Sheet

1. _____
2. _____
3. □ Male □ Female
4. _____
5. _____
6. _____
7. □ Yes □ No
8. _____

9. □ Yes □ No
10. □ Yes □ No
11.
12. □ Yes □ No
13. □ Yes □ No
14. □ Yes □ No
15. □ Yes □ No
16. □ Yes □ No
17. □ Yes □ No
18. □ Yes □ No
19. □ Yes □ No
20. □ Yes □ No
21. □ Yes □ No
22. □ Yes □ No
23. □ Yes □ No
24. □ Yes □ No
25. □ Yes □ No
26. □ Yes □ No
27. □ Yes □ No
28. □ Yes □ No
29. □ Yes □ No

30. □ Yes □ No
31. □ Yes □ No
32. □ Yes □ No
33. □ Yes □ No
34. □ Yes □ No
35. □ Yes □ No
36. □ Yes □ No
37. □ Yes □ No
38. a. □ Yes □ No
    b. □ Yes □ No
    c. □ Yes □ No
    d. □ Yes □ No
    e. □ Yes □ No
    f. □ Yes □ No
    g. □ Yes □ No
    h. □ Yes □ No
    i. □ Yes □ No
    j. □ Yes □ No
    k. □ Yes □ No
    l. □ Yes □ No
    m. □ Yes □ No
39. a. Less than once a year
    b. About once a year
    c. About two or three times a year
    d. About once a month
    e. About two or three times a month
    f. About once a week
    g. About two or three times a week
    h. Every day or almost every day

40. □ Yes □ No
41. a. Nearly every time
    b. More than half the time
    c. Less than half the time
    d. Once in a while
    e. Never
42. a. Never
    b. Less than once a year
    c. About once a year
    d. About two or three times a year
    e. About once a month
    f. About two or three times a month
    g. About once a week
    h. About two or three times a week
    i. Every day or almost every day
43. □ Yes □ No
44.
45. □ Yes □ No
46. □ Yes □ No
47. □ Yes □ No
48. □ Yes □ No
49. □ Yes □ No
50. □ Yes □ No
51. □ Yes □ No
52. □ Yes □ No
53. □ Yes □ No
54. □ Yes □ No
55. □ Yes □ No
56. □ Yes □ No

57. □ Yes □ No
58. □ Yes □ No
59. □ Yes □ No
60. □ Yes □ No
61. □ Yes □ No
62. □ Yes □ No
63. □ Yes □ No
64. □ Yes □ No
65. □ Yes □ No
66. □ Yes □ No
67. □ Yes □ No
68. □ Yes □ No
69. □ Yes □ No
70. □ Yes □ No
71. □ Yes □ No
72. □ Yes □ No
73. □ Yes □ No
74. □ Yes □ No
75. □ Yes □ No
76. □ Yes □ No
77. □ Yes □ No
78. □ Yes □ No
79. □ Yes □ No
80. □ Yes □ No

Appendix C:
Definitions of Drinking and Problem Drinking Measures

Definitions of Drinking and Problem Drinking Measures

Drinking Measures

Q_1 *Sample.* For the Pilot Questionnaire, drinker status was determined by a response of more frequently than "never" on the frequency of drinking item (No. 20). Correlations of social/attitudinal items with drinking, to determine predictors of drinking incidence (Column 2, Tables 6 and 7), were made on the basis of computing rs between the predictor items and Item No. 20 (drinking frequency) for the total sample.

Q_2 *Sample.* For the Youth Drinking Questionnaire (Q_2), drinker status was determined by an affirmative response to Item No. 37 ("Had a drink more than two or three times in your life"). All correlations with predictor items upon drinker status (Column 2, Tables 6 and 7) entailed computing rs between the predictor items and the dichotomous Item No. 37.

Quantity x Frequency Classification. For purposes of the quantity x frequency classification used in Table 5, the following criteria were employed in defining the classes. "Abstainers" drank less than once per year (Item No. 39). "Infrequent drinkers" drank less than once a month but at least once a year. The remaining classes employed both the drinking frequency item (No. 39) and the usual quantity item (No. 44). "Light drinkers" had one or two drinks about once a month or two or three times a month, *or* had one drink one to three times a week or every day. "Moderate drinkers" had at least three drinks about once a month, three or four drinks two or three times a month, or two drinks one to three times a week or daily. "Heavy drinkers" had at least five drinks two or three times a month, or at least three drinks one to three times a week or daily.

Problem Drinking Measures

Q_1 *Sample.* The "style component" of problem drinking was a three-category scale (0, 1, 2) where "0" was defined as affirming no style items, "1" as affirming 1-3 style items, and "2" as affirming at least 4 style items. The pool of 16 style items were Item Nos. 23, 25, 26, 28-32, 36, 38, 40, 42, 43, 45, 46, and 56.

The "consumption component" was defined as a three-category scale (0, 1, 2), based on the response to the frequency item (No. 20) and the quantity item (No. 53; "When you drink, do you have more than two or three of whatever you're drinking"). "0" was defined as drinking not more than two or three drinks once a month or less. "1" was defined as drinking once a week or more, but drinking not more than two or three drinks per occasion. "2" was defined as drinking once a week or more and drinking more than two or three drinks per occasion.

The "consequences component" was defined as a three-category scale (0, 1, 2), based on a pool of seven items (Nos. 21, 27, 34, 35, 37, 39, and 44). "0" was defined as affirming none of the seven items; "1" as affirming one of the seven items; and "2" as affirming at least two of the seven items.

Q_2 *Sample.* The three problem drinking components were defined (for drinkers) as follows: "Style" (0, 1, 2) was defined on the basis of the item pool, Nos. 31, 38a, b, d, e, f, g, h, i, j, k, 47-66, 77, 78, "Gets drunk at least once a month" from 39, and "Gets high at least more than half the time" from No. 41. "0" was defined as affirming none of the items, "1" as affirming one to four of the items, and "2" as affirming at least five of the items.

"Consumption" (0, 1, 2) was defined on the basis of the frequency item (No. 39) and the quantity item (No. 44). "0" was defined as seven or fewer drinks once a month or less, "1" was defined as four or fewer drinks two or three times a month or more, and "2" was defined as eight or more drinks once a month or less *or* five or more drinks two or three times a month or more.

"Consequences" (0, 1, 2) was defined on the basis of the item pool, Nos. 67-76, and 79. "0" was defined as affirming none of the items, "1" as affirming one of the items, and "2" as affirming at least two of the items.

Overall Problems Typology. While the above measures were defined for drinkers only, the overall problems typology (0, 1, 2, 3, 4) (Table 13) was defined for the total Q_2 Sample. "0" was defined as drinking less frequently than once per year. "1" was defined as drinking at least once per year, but not once a month. "2" was defined as consumption >0 or consequences >0, but not in "3" or "4". "3" was defined as affirming either of the binge drinking items (No. 61 or 62) or having consumption $= 2$. "4" was defined as having consequences $= 2$.

About the Author

Tom Alibrandi, as Director of Youth Services for the Alcoholism Council of Orange County in California, worked with minors who had been diverted by the juvenile justice system as first-time and chronic alcohol abusers. He counseled out-of-control minor dependents and their parents for Orange County's Family Development Program. He also taught a creative writing course in journal-keeping to residents of a treatment program.

A graduate of Syracuse University, certified as a counselor in alcoholism and related disorders from the University of California in Los Angeles, he has served as special consultant to the State of California Office of Alcoholism.

He has taught and lectured at several colleges and universities in California and is the author of several magazine articles and eight other books: *Free Yourself; The Meditation Handbook; Biorhythm—Get the Most Out of Your Life* (all published by Major Books); *Hallways,* a book of poetry, from Chicken Walk; *Killshot; Uncle Joe Shannon* and *Custody* by Pinnacle Books, and *The Constructor* from Delacorte Press.

His documentary film, *Young Alcoholics,* TGB Productions, is based on this book.

About the Author

CompCare® publications

A Division of the Comprehensive Care Corporation
Post Office Box 27777, Minneapolis, Minnesota 55427

for faster service on charge orders
call us toll free at:

800/328-3330

In Minnesota, call collect 612/559-4800

ORDER FORM

Date _____

Order Number	Customer Number	Customer P.O.	☐ ☐ ☐ ☐ ☐ 1 2 3 4 5	For Office Use Only

UPS 1 ☐	PP 2 ☐	PPD 3 ☐	PPD CHGS 4 ☐	WILL CALL 5 ☐	OUR TRUCK 6 ☐	CARRIER

BILL ORDER TO:

Name _____

Address _____

City / State / Zip _____

Non-profit organization, please show tax exemption number [_____]

Signature _____   Sales and use tax number _____

SHIP ORDER TO: (If other than above)

Name _____

Address _____

City / State / Zip _____

Telephone _____   Purchase Order (if required) _____

☐ Please ship back-ordered items as soon as possible

☐ Please cancel order for items out of stock

☐ Please send _____ copies of *Young Alcoholics* at $6.50 each. (Catalog number 03053.)

☐ Please send me the CompCare Catalog of more books and materials for growth-centered living. (No charge.)

PLEASE FILL IN BELOW FOR CHARGE ORDERS
Or enclose check for total amount of order.

Prices subject to change without notice.

Account No (12 or more digits) from your credit card

Check one.

☐ VISA   ☐ MASTER CHARGE   Master Charge—also enter 4
                                    digits below your account no

Your Card
Issuing Bank _____   Expiration
                                Date of Card _____

Credit Card
Signature _____

TOTAL PRICE _____

4% Sales Tax _____
(Minnesota residents only)

Postage & Handling charge _____
Add 75 cents to orders totaling less than $15.00
Add 5% to orders totaling $15.00 or more

GRAND TOTAL _____
(U.S. Dollars)

All orders shipped outside continental
U.S.A. will be billed actual shipping costs.

VISA®   master charge

CompCare®
publications

A Division of the Comprehensive Care Corporation
Post Office Box 27777, Minneapolis, Minnesota 55427

for faster service on charge orders
call us toll free at:

800/328-3330

In Minnesota, call collect 612/559-4800

ORDER FORM

Date _____

Order Number	Customer Number	Customer P.O.	☐ ☐ ☐ ☐ ☐ 1 2 3 4 5	**For Office Use Only**

| UPS
1
☐ | PP
2
☐ | PPD
3
☐ | PPD
CHGS
4
☐ | WILL
CALL
5
☐ | OUR
TRUCK
6
☐ | CARRIER
_____ |

BILL ORDER TO:

Name _____

Address _____

City/State/Zip _____

Non-profit organization, please show tax exemption number [   ]

Signature _____ Sales and use tax number _____

SHIP ORDER TO: (If other than above)

Name _____

Address _____

City/State/Zip _____

Telephone _____ Purchase Order (if required)_____

☐ Please ship back-ordered items as soon as possible

☐ Please cancel order for items out of stock

☐ Please send _____ copies of *Young Alcoholics* at $6.50 each. (Catalog number 03053.)

☐ Please send me the CompCare Catalog of more books and materials for growth-centered living. (No charge.)

PLEASE FILL IN BELOW FOR CHARGE ORDERS
Or enclose check for total amount of order.

Prices subject to change without notice.

Account No. (12 or more digits) from your credit card

[☐☐☐☐☐☐☐☐☐☐☐☐☐☐☐☐☐]   [☐☐☐☐]

Check one:
☐ VISA   ☐ MASTER CHARGE   Master Charge—also enter 4
                                   digits below your account no.

| Your Card
Issuing Bank | _____ | Expiration
Date of Card _____ |

Credit Card
Signature _____

TOTAL PRICE _____

4% Sales Tax _____
(Minnesota residents only)

Postage & Handling charge _____
Add 75 cents to orders totaling less than $15.00
Add 5% to orders totaling $15.00 or more

GRAND TOTAL _____
(U.S. Dollars)

All orders shipped outside continental
U.S.A. will be billed actual shipping costs.

VISA®   master charge